SOP for Conducting Marine Bird and Mammal Surveys — Version 4.1

Southwest Alaska Inventory and Monitoring Network

Natural Resource Report NPS/SWAN/NRR—2011/392

James L. Bodkin[1]

[1]U.S. Geological Survey
Alaska Science Center,
4210 University Drive
Anchorage, AK 99508

May 2011

U.S. Department of the Interior
National Park Service
Natural Resource Program Center
Fort Collins, Colorado

The National Park Service, Natural Resource Program Center publishes a range of reports that address natural resource topics of interest and applicability to a broad audience in the National Park Service and others in natural resource management, including scientists, conservation and environmental constituencies, and the public.

The Natural Resource Report Series is used to disseminate high-priority, current natural resource management information with managerial application. The series targets a general, diverse audience, and may contain NPS policy considerations or address sensitive issues of management applicability.

All manuscripts in the series receive the appropriate level of peer review to ensure that the information is scientifically credible, technically accurate, appropriately written for the intended audience, and designed and published in a professional manner. This report received formal peer review by subject-matter experts who were not directly involved in the collection, analysis, or reporting of the data, and whose background and expertise put them on par technically and scientifically with the authors of the information.

Views, statements, findings, conclusions, recommendations, and data in this report are those of the author(s) and do not necessarily reflect views and policies of the National Park Service, U.S. Department of the Interior. Mention of trade names or commercial products does not constitute endorsement or recommendation for use by the National Park Service.

This report is available from the Southwest Alaska Inventory & Monitoring Network website (http://science.nature.nps.gov/im/units/swan/) and the Natural Resource Publications Management website (http://www.nature.nps.gov/publications/nrpm/).

Please cite this publication as:

Bodkin, J. L. SOP for conducting marine bird and mammal surveys - Version 4.1: Southwest Alaska Inventory and Monitoring Network. Natural Resource Report NPS/SWAN/NRR— 2011/392. National Park Service, Fort Collins, Colorado.

NPS 953/107687, May 2011

Revision History Log

All edits and amendments made to this document since its inception should be recorded in the table below. Users of this protocol should promptly notify the project leader of the marine nearshore monitoring program of recommended edits or changes. The project leader will review and incorporate suggested changes as necessary, record these changes in the revision history log, and modify the date and version number on the title page of this document to reflect these changes.

Revision History Log:

Previous Version #	Revision Date	Author	Changes Made	Reason for Change	New Version #
Version 4.0	08/19/2010	Coletti	Formatting; updating to reflect SWAN	To meet NRR standards	Version 4.1
Version 4.1	3/21/2011	Bodkin	Final edit		4.1
Add rows as needed for each change or set of changes associated with each version.					

Contents

Contents (continued)

Figures

Tables

Appendices

1 Background and Objectives

1.1 Introduction

The purpose of this SOP is to describe the justification, sampling design and process for collecting, recording, and analyzing data to estimate the relative abundance of nearshore, or coastal marine birds and mammals under the National Park Service Vital Signs Monitoring program in the Gulf of Alaska. The surveys described are vessel based and observers identify and count all birds and mammals that are detected within strip transects that extend from the shoreline offshore for 200 m. The results of the surveys will provide estimates of the species composition, relative abundance, and distribution of all marine birds and mammals within this nearshore zone. The focus of these surveys will be on marine birds that are trophically linked to the kelp/benthic invertebrate nearshore food web, and include species of sea ducks (Harlequin ducks, Barrow's and common goldeneye, bufflehead, long-tail ducks, and scoters), mergansers (common and red-breasted), and shorebirds, specifically the black oystercatcher (see Black Oystercatcher SOP). Because other birds and mammals will be encountered in the course of these surveys, observations of all marine birds and mammals will be recorded.

1.2 Rationale for conducting marine bird and mammal surveys

The sea ducks, and black oystercatcher were selected for focus because of their reliance on habitats and prey associated with the nearshore communities that are the focus of the SWAN Monitoring program. These species are top level consumers of nearshore marine invertebrates such as mussels, clams, snails, limpets, and barnacles that are being monitored under the SWAN invertebrate and algal sampling SOP. Because these bird species are recognized to play important roles as consumers of marine invertebrates (Draulans 1982, Marsh 1986, Meire 1993, Lindberg et al. 1998, Hamilton and Nudds 2003), understanding cause of change in abundance over time of these consumers will be facilitated through the direct estimates of their prey populations provided through the SWAN monitoring program. Moreover, monitoring trends in abundance of the various guilds of marine birds, e.g. the alcids, loons, grebes, gulls, and cormorants that occupy other food webs or habitats may improve the ability to discriminate among potential causes of change in trends. For example, concurrent changes in sea ducks that forage on nearshore invertebrates, and the alcids that forage on zooplankton or small schooling fish may suggest a common cause of change, one that may be independent of food. Such an approach may provide insights related to competing hypothesis relative to cause of change within or among populations (Petersen et al. 2003). In addition many of these species, including the Harlequin duck, Barrow's goldeneye, and black oystercatcher were impacted by the *Exxon Valdez* oil spill, and exhibited protracted recovery periods as a consequence of lingering oil in nearshore habitats in Prince William Sound (Andres 1999, Trust et al. 2000, Esler et al. 2000, Esler et al. 2002). Long-term monitoring of these species will likely provide increased confidence in assessment of the status of these populations relative to restoration and recovery from the 1989 spill. Additionally, existing data collected using comparable methods are available from areas in the Gulf of Alaska for periods up to 20 years (Irons et al.1988, Irons et al. 2000). Because this protocol focuses on species associated with nearshore intertidal and subtidal habitats, species of marine birds and mammals that occur further offshore will be underrepresented. We anticipate that development of monitoring protocols for the Alaska Coastal Current through the EVOS Long Term Monitoring program will incorporate surveys of species of birds and mammals that are prevalent offshore and that those surveys will be coordinated with the nearshore surveys we describe here. The distribution of most marine birds and mammals includes habitats that extend beyond 200 m from shore, thus estimates derived from these surveys will be improved by including sampling of offshore areas. Because sea otters are another nearshore focal species and are known to regularly occur far from shore in waters > 100 m in depth (Bodkin and Udevitz 1999) and display avoidance behaviors to vessels that reduces detection (Udevitz et al. 1995), a specific aerial survey will be employed by the SWAN Monitoring Program to estimate their abundance (see Sea Otter Aerial Survey SOP).

1.3 Measurable Objective

Specifically, the objectives of this task are to assess changes in:

- Estimate long-term trends in the seasonal abundance of seabirds and sea ducks in both summer and winter seasons

2 Sampling Design

2.2 Sampling Design Overview

The proposed survey design will allow estimation of nearshore marine bird and mammal densities and abundances at the level of the park every year. From a series of contiguous transects that cover all shorelines, including islands, a systematically selected set of transects, from a random start point are selected for sampling a systematic sampling of 200 m wide transects perpendicular and contiguous with the shore will be employed to estimate the abundance and species composition of marine birds and marine mammals annually within a park in the summer (June/July) and biennially in late winter (March) (See SWAN Protocol Narrative section Dean and Bodkin 2011). The summer and winter surveys will systematically sample approximately 20% of all shoreline habitat within each park. The survey sampling unit is a strip transect, up to 5 km long by 200 m wide by 100 m high that is centered 100 m offshore of the sea water tidal level at the time the survey is conducted. Transects are systematically selected from the pool of contiguous 5 km transects that are adjacent to the mainland or islands, plus the lengths of transects that are associated with islands or groups of islands with less than 5 km of shoreline.

The survey vessel will have a set of maps suitable for locating and sampling each transect and a computer and Global Positioning System (GPS) with the survey software dLOG2 (R.G. Ford Consulting Co., Portland, OR) that will visually display the shoreline, the transect line, including endpoints, and the survey vessel location. Additionally the survey vessel will have a list of the end points for each transect and a set of maps suitable for navigating and sampling each transect. Transect endpoints and survey data waypoints will be entered, stored, and managed in ArcGIS (ESRI, Redlands, CA).

The surveys will be based from a dedicated support vessel or from smaller vessels as conditions and season require. To minimize the potential effects of seasonal movements, surveys will be conducted during the same 2-3 week period each year.

Surveys are conducted from vessels that are navigated along selected sections of coastline that represent independent transects. Transect width is 200 m and two observers search each side of the vessel out 100 m. All marine birds and mammals are identified and counted within the 200 m transect width that includes 100 m ahead of, behind, and over the vessel. One observer navigates the skiff, and preferably surveys the offshore portion of the transect. The second observer counts birds and mammals on the shore side of the survey transect, and a third member of the team is responsible for entering observations into a computer program (dLOG2) designed specifically for these surveys (Appendix A). dLOG2 is a data logging and real time mapping program that plots track lines and user generated data against user defined baseline maps, during data collection. Position data are read from an onboard GPS connected to the host computer. All data are written continuously to the hard disk for back-up at days end.

From a series of contiguous transects that cover all shorelines, including islands, a systematically selected set of transects, from a random start point are selected for sampling. The survey vessel (typically from 6-20 m in length) with good forward and lateral viewing for two observers travels at a speed of 8-12 knots along the transect. Observers scan each side of the vessel from the bow to the stern, and provide to the data recorder the numbers, species, and activity of all marine birds and mammals detected. Data are entered by a data recorder directly into a portable computer using a software program designed specifically for these types of surveys (dLOG2). The computer keypad consists of "hot keys" that code for species, and activity, and the data recorder enters the number of individuals associated with each sighting. Completion of the transect is noted and recorded in dLOG2 and on the transect log by the data recorder who is visually monitoring the progress of the vessel along the transect, and informs the observers of the transect's end.

2.2 Rationale for Selecting this Sampling Design over Others
The proposed survey design will allow estimation of nearshore marine bird and mammal densities and abundances at the level of the park every year. Survey results will be comparable across Southwest Alaska Network (SWAN) regions, and will be comparable with historic surveys using similar methodologies. Although the Swan Monitoring Program's focus is on species of birds and mammals trophically linked to shallow water habitats (i.e. sea otter, sea ducks, black oystercatchers), occurrences of all species of marine birds and mammals will be recorded during the survey. Historic data collected using this method have proven useful in detecting status and trends among many of the marine birds common in the Gulf of Alaska (Irons et al. 2000, Lance et al. 2001). The survey design employs sensitivity and optimization analyses of data collected using similar methodologies in Prince William Sound, Alaska (West 2003) and in Glacier Bay (J. Bodkin unpublished data) over multiple years (see section 2.4).

2.2 Choosing Sampling Units
The rational for selection of the park unit, as the primary sampling unit for marine birds is based on two factors. One is the availability of intertidal invertebrate and algal measurements from the intensive sampling sites within the same park units that the bird and mammal surveys will be completed. This nested design will provide increased power to detect significant correlations between invertebrate prey and vertebrate predator status and trends in abundances over time. Power to detect correlations would likely be diminished, based on higher variances associated with the lower sampling intensity required if the sample unit for both invertebrates and vertebrates were at a larger scale. The second factor, related to the first, is the appropriate spatial scale at which to sample marine birds and mammals. Because of their potential mobility, the sample unit should be of sufficient size to minimize the potentially confounding effects of movements of species across sample unit boundaries between survey periods. For our suite of focal species, but not all species of marine birds, and probably few of the marine mammals, the sample unit of the park is large enough to minimize the effects of movements during the periods of sampling.

2.3 Recommended Frequency and Timing of Sampling
Surveys of marine birds and mammals will be conducted annually in each park unit during the summer months (June/July) and biennially for each park unit during the winter months (February/March). This sampling frequency will allow detection of species composition and abundance of species that reside year round, as well as those that over-winter in nearshore habitats in the Gulf of Alaska, but may be absent, or in reduced densities during the summer breeding period (e.g. Harlequin ducks, Barrows goldeneye and bufflehead).

2.4 Level of Change that can be Detected

As indicated in the SWAN Protocol Narrative (Dean and Bodkin 2011) the objective of the marine bird and mammal surveys is to assess how estimates of abundance change over time and how those changes vary with respect to location. The levels of change that we can expect to detect and the time and spatial scales over which they are to be detected vary with metric. In general, the goal for most biological metrics (e.g. abundance of sea otters, harlequin ducks, or dominant intertidal invertebrates like mussels) is to detect levels of change that are deemed to be of ecological importance (Dean and Bodkin 2011). In the case of most nearshore marine birds a change of 50% or more is considered ecologically significant.

The ability to detect change can be expressed as power, the probability that a given level of change could be detected given the sampling design employed. Power analyses can also be used as a planning tool, to determine the sampling effort required to detect a given level of change with a prescribed power. It may be possible to make a reasonable approximation of power for each metric by estimating ranges of means and variances, based in part on data from elsewhere, and then performing simulations to estimate a range in levels of detectable change that might be expected. However, these have not been performed to date because such an effort is outside of the current scope of work. It is suggested that the appropriate power analyses be performed as data are gathered (after five years, and at five year intervals thereafter) to determine the power to detect changes and to modify sampling designs as required. These changes might suggest reducing sampling effort to achieve greater efficiency or increasing sampling effort in order to achieve reasonable power to detect change.

It is reasonable to assume that the power required to detect a given level of change will increase over time as the number of surveys increases. This again stresses the need for conducting periodic power analyses to suggest modifications to sampling designs over time and to ensure efficiency in the sampling.

3 Field Season

3.1 Overview and General Methods

See Appendix B and Appendix C for a description of the field methods from which this protocol was derived.

From vessels that navigate transects located 100m offshore of the sea land interface at the time of the survey, pairs of observers search, identify, count, and record all marine birds and mammals detected within transect bounds. Survey vessels travel at approximately 10 knots, but survey speed can vary from nearly stopped when birds are abundant and species diverse, to speeds up to 12 knots when transects are straight lines birds and mammals are rare. Sightings are recorded by a third crew member directly into dLOG2, (Appendix A) a survey and data entry program developed specifically for this type of survey. The number and species or taxa, and their habitat (flying, water, or land) and foraging behavior, at the time of detection (or prior to disturbance if it can be inferred, e.g. a bird flushed off the water) are entered by the recorder. The survey design incorporates a systematic sampling of a series of transects, each up to 5 km in length, located within the Parks, and adjacent to all shorelines including offshore islands and islets, up to 2 km offshore.

The sampling unit is the individual transect. The transect is defined by endpoints located 100 m offshore and a line that extends between those endpoints and remains 100 m offshore along its length. The area surveyed along the transect includes the space that extends 100 m from each side, 100 m ahead of and behind, and 100 m above the boat. The three-dimensional space created by these dimensions is known as the "sampling window." The set of transects identified within each intensive block and region represent the samples from which population estimates and variances will be calculated.

3.2 Observer Condition

Weather and sea conditions can affect detection of birds and mammals from vessels at sea. In general winds and sea state (Beaufort index) are inversely related to detection. (Gould and Forsell 1989) calm seas and wind and unrestricted visibility generally offer the best survey conditions, and as wind, sea, swell, increase and visibility decreases (e.g. fog or darkness) viewing conditions deteriorate, largely as a function of reduced detection that may not be equivalent among all species being surveyed. Therefore it is important to limit surveys to periods when viewing conditions are fair or better. In general wind velocities consistently > 15 knots and sea conditions > Beaufort 3 are not suitable for surveying (Table 1), and Beaufort numbers of 0-2 are preferable. On occasion local environmental conditions may result in unsuitable observation conditions. In these instances transects should not be surveyed, but rather should be omitted. Not more than 10% of the transects should be omitted due to poor observation conditions.

Table 1. Beaufort Sea state scale

Beaufort number (force)	Wind Speed		Wave height (feet)	WMO* description	Effects observed on the sea
	knots	mph			
0	under 1	under 1	-	**Calm**	Sea is like a mirror
1	1 - 3	1 - 3	0.25	**Light air**	Ripples with appearance of scales; no foam crests
2	4 - 6	4 - 7	0.5 - 1	**Light breeze**	Small wavelets; crests of glassy appearance, not breaking
3	7 - 10	8 - 12	2 - 3	**Gentle breeze**	Large wavelets; crests begin to break; scattered whitecaps
4	11-16	13-18	3½ - 5	**Moderate breeze**	Small waves, becoming longer; numerous whitecaps
5	17-21	19-24	6 - 8	**Fresh breeze**	Moderate waves, taking longer form; many whitecaps; some spray
6	22-27	25-31	9½-13	**Strong breeze**	Larger waves forming; whitecaps everywhere; more spray
7	28-33	32-38	13½-19	**Near gale**	Sea heaps up; white foam from breaking waves begins to be blown in streaks
8	34-40	39-46	18-25	**Gale**	Moderately high waves of greater length; edges of crests begin to break into spindrift; foam is blown in well-marked streaks
9	41-47	47-54	23-32	**Strong gale**	High waves; sea begins to roll; dense streaks of foam; spray may begin to reduce visibility
10	48-55	55-63	29-41	**Storm**	Very high waves with overhanging crests; sea takes white appearance as foam is blown in very dense streaks; rolling is heavy and visibility is reduced
11	56-63	64-72	37-52	**Violent storm**	Exceptionally high waves; sea covered with white foam patches; visibility further reduced
12	64 and over	73 and over	45 and over	**Hurricane**	Air filled with foam; sea completely white with driving spray; visibility greatly reduced

3.3 Field Season Preparation

Prior to each field season, the following tasks are to be performed.

- Review the master field schedule and prepare a list of tasks to be performed and set the field schedule

- Review personnel requirements, train personnel as needed, and make personnel assignments
- Arrange for vessel charters as needed
- Prepare an itinerary and emergency contact list
- Assemble and distribute personal emergency safety equipment
- Arrange for travel of personnel to the departure site
- Prepare survey vessels for use, including operational and safety equipment
- Review sampling procedures
- Gather equipment and supplies including
  o Laptop computer with survey software (dLOG2, Portland Or), shoreline and transect GIS files, data entry forms (Transect log, Transect checklist), prior marine bird and mammal databases and reports, standard operating procedures, and other required software loaded
  o Digital camera and accessories (memory sticks, cables for downloading images to a computer)
  o GPS with local charts loaded
  o Printed copies of transect maps at a resolution adequate to aid in navigation between endpoints in the event of GPS failure
  o Field guides to marine birds and mammals (Sibley 2000, Armstrong 1996, Wynn 1997)
  o High resolution binoculars (10 x 42 Leica recommended), 1 pair/observer
  o Data sheets to include hard copies of Transect log, Transect checklists, Survey data codes and species codes for all marine birds and mammals
  o Batteries and battery chargers for electronics
  o Pencils, clipboards, permanent markers, and misc. office supplies
- Ensure that electronics have fresh batteries and are in good working order

3.4 Sequence of Events

Surveys of marine birds and mammals will be conducted annually during the summer. Surveys will be conducted biennially in late winter to sample over wintering species. Winter surveys will occur in late February - March and summer surveys in June/July. Surveys will be conducted from vessels that afford good forward, lateral, and aft viewing and capable of safely navigating defined transects. Sampling of transects will generally occur in a spatially systematic way to minimize the amount of time that elapses between sampling of individual transects and that minimizes the time required to sample all transects. Personnel may be supported by a larger vessel that provides lodging and meals, or from smaller survey vessels.

3.5 Details of Data Collection

Prior to beginning the survey the observers and data recorders should review this SOP. The survey should be conducted during the same 2-3 week period as in prior surveys of similar design and only under environmental and operational conditions described in this SOP. Marine bird and mammal number and location data are recorded directly into an electronic data base (dLOG2) at the time of data collection. The order of transect completion may vary over time, largely dependent on logistics and weather conditions but all transects should be completed for each survey and in a way that minimizes the potentially confounding effects of movements of individuals among transects. Transects that are not surveyed are deleted from the sample during analysis, reducing the area sampled, but not the sample area. On a daily basis, following survey work, survey data should be reviewed for completeness and accuracy. Data should be backed up on a daily basis and stored away from the original data.

3.5.1 Transect Log

Prior to the start of each transect, transect attribute data are entered into the Transect log (Table 2), that includes date, recorders initials, transect #, file name for each transect. File names will include the 2-3 character code for the region being surveyed (e.g. PWS, KP, KOD, and AP), the 1-2 character number of the intensive block (1-12) if applicable, followed by the date (day/month/year: dd/mm/year), the transect number (up to 3 numbers), followed by the season (w for winter, and s for summer). As an example AP 10 13072006 22 S.srv represents the file name assigned to transect 22 in the intensive block 10 along the Alaska Peninsula coast sampled on 13 July 2006. This log is used to verify transect data in dLOG2 and to make note of errors that will later require editing of electronic files. Accurate recording of start and stop transect times and transect numbers are essential. It may be necessary to go "off transect" prior to completing a transect (e.g. to identify and count a complex flock of birds or a rare marine mammal, or for other navigational purposes). The transect log should be used to record these times as well as using the "off "and "on" transect keys in dLOG2. The off transect key in dLOG2 should also be used to record sightings of all marine mammals or other unusual observations that are beyond the sampling window of the transect. Comments on unusual sightings or occurrences are encouraged and can be entered directly into the dLOG2 comments field or in the transect log to later be appended to the transect data file.

Table 2. Transect Log data sheet used to verify transect start, stop, and completion and to record required edits to the electronic files and file names of each transect.

Transect no._22_____

MB&M Survey recorder__**JBodkin**_____

Page _____

Survey Date: _dd/mm/year (ex:13072006)_____

Season (circle one): __Winter_____Summer____

Format for Naming .SRV output files: example:_AP 10 13072006 22 w_____

Region: _AP_____Block no._10_____

Date	Boat Name	Transect #	File Name	Start Time	Stop Time	Proofed	Comments

Please be accurate with times.

Please cross-off comments if fixed during proofing.

Environmental and observer data are recorded directly into dLOG2 for each transect surveyed. These data include the unique trip ID#, the Beaufort sea conditions at the time of the survey for each transect, present observer viewing conditions along the inshore and offshore portions of the transect, the marine habitat zone (always shoreline) sea conditions, and the observers name (3 letter initials) and location (inshore or offshore) (Table 3).

Table 3 Other Codes of observer and sea conditions
Codes for observer and sea conditions:

Observer Conditions	
1	excellent
2	very good
3	good
4	fair
5	poor
Sea Conditions	
0	flat calm
1	rippled
2	up to 6 inch chop
3	up to 1 foot chop
4	1 - 2 foot chop
5	2 - 4 foot chop
6	4 - 6 foot chop
7	6 - 8 foot chop

Transect data and environmental and observer data are entered prior to initiation of the transect. Once these data are entered and the vessel has navigated to one of the endpoints of the transect, the recorder notes the start transect time on the transect log and hits the "On-Tx" key in the dLOG2 program, and informs the observers that they are now "on transect".

3.5.2 Transect Data
Once the transect has begun, each observer should be carefully scanning, with the aid of binoculars as necessary, the sampling window on their side of the vessels. Usually the vessel operator should be searching the seaward side of the transect and the other observer the shoreward side of the transect. Because bird densities will usually be greater on the shoreward side of the transect this facilitates the vessel operators safe and accurate navigation. The data recorder may aid in searching and all observers have the latitude to search the entire sampling window. Observers report to the recorder the species, number, behavior, and habitat, where applicable, of all marine birds and mammals detected within the sampling window (Tables 4 and 5). Observations of marine mammals or other noteworthy observations outside the sampling widow should be recorded as "Off-TX" in dLOG2. The recorder enters the species code either directly or by striking the "hot key" representing that species.

3.5.3 Species
Table 4 lists the birds and mammals that are likely to be encountered during these surveys. Species identifications should be made to the lowest possible taxa, but identifications must be made based on the identifying characteristics of each sighting. Care should be taken in each identification and it may be possible to only identify a species to genus or some other higher

classification (see the discussion in Appendix B pg 12-13). In the case of sea otters (SEOT) adults and dependent pups are recorded independently.

Table 4 Species Codes

Codes for species observed during marine bird and mammal surveys. Note that not all species have been observed in all regions. The list originated during pelagic surveys in Cook Inlet and has since been expanded to include species observed in the Gulf of Alaska.

GROUP	ABBREVIATION	SPECIES
ALCID	ANMU	Ancient Murrelet
ALCID	BRMU	Brachyramphus Murrelet
ALCID	CAAU	Cassin's Auklet
ALCID	COMU	Common Murre
ALCID	CRAU	Crested Auklet
ALCID	HOPU	Horned Puffin
ALCID	KIMU	Kittlitz's Murrelet
ALCID	LEAU	Least Auklet
ALCID	MAMU	Marbled Murrelet
ALCID	PAAU	Parakeet Auklet
ALCID	PIGU	Pigeon Guillemot
ALCID	RHAU	Rhinocerous Auklet
ALCID	TBMU	Thick-billed Murre
ALCID	TUPU	Tufted Puffin
ALCID	UNAC	Unidentified Alcid
ALCID	UNAU	Unidentified Auklet
ALCID	UNMU	Unidentified Murre
ALCID	WHAU	Whiskered Auklet
CORMORANT	BRAC	Brant's Cormorant
CORMORANT	DCCO	Double-crested Cormorant
CORMORANT	PECO	Pelagic Cormorant
CORMORANT	RFCO	Red-faced Cormorant
CORMORANT	UNCO	Unidentified Cormorant
DUCK	AMWI	American Wigeon
DUCK	BAGO	Barrow's Goldeneye
DUCK	BLSC	Black Scoter
DUCK	BUFF	Bufflehead
DUCK	COEI	Common Eider
DUCK	COGO	Common Goldeneye
DUCK	COME	Common Merganser
DUCK	GADW	Gadwall
DUCK	GRSC	Greater Scaup

GROUP	ABBREVIATION	SPECIES
DUCK	GWTE	Green-winged Teal
DUCK	HADU	Harlequin Duck
DUCK	LESC	Lesser Scaup
DUCK	MALL	Mallard
DUCK	NOPI	Northern Pintail
DUCK	NOSH	Northern Shoveler
DUCK	OLDS	Oldsquaw
DUCK	RBME	Red-breasted Merganser
DUCK	SCAU	Scaup
DUCK	SUSC	Surf Scoter
DUCK	UNDU	Unidentified Duck
DUCK	UNGO	Unidentified Goldeneye
DUCK	UNME	Unidentified Merganser
DUCK	UNSC	Unidentified Scoter
DUCK	UNTL	Unidentified Teal
DUCK	WWSC	White-winged Scoter
GOOSE	BRAN	Brant
GOOSE	CAGO	Canada Goose
GOOSE	UNSN	Unidentified Swan
GREBE	HOGR	Horned Grebe
GREBE	RNGR	Red-necked Grebe
GREBE	UNGR	Unidentified Grebe
GULL	BLKI	Black-legged Kittiwake
GULL	BOGU	Bonaparte's Gull
GULL	GLGU	Glaucous Gull
GULL	GWGU	Glaucous-winged Gull
GULL	HEGU	Herring Gull
GULL	IVGU	Ivory Gull
GULL	MEGU	Mew Gull
GULL	RBGU	Ring-billed Gull
GULL	RLKI	Red-legged Kittiwake
GULL	ROGU	Ross' Gull
GULL	SAGU	Sabine's Gull
GULL	THGU	Thayer's Gull
GULL	UNGU	Unidentified Gull
GULL	UNLL	Unidentified Large Larid
JAEGER	LTJA	Long-tailed Jaeger
JAEGER	PAJA	Parasitic Jaeger
JAEGER	POJA	Pomarine Jaeger
JAEGER	UNJA	Unidentified Jaeger

GROUP	ABBREVIATION	SPECIES
LOON	COLO	Common Loon
LOON	PALO	Pacific Loon
LOON	RTLO	Red-throated Loon
LOON	UNLO	Unidentified Loon
LOON	YBLO	Yellow-billed Loon
MARINE MAMMAL	DAPO	Dall's Porpoise
MARINE MAMMAL	FIWH	Fin Whale
MARINE MAMMAL	HAPO	Harbor Porpoise
MARINE MAMMAL	HASE	Harbor Seal
MARINE MAMMAL	HUWH	Humpback Whale
MARINE MAMMAL	KIWH	Killer Whale
MARINE MAMMAL	MIWH	Minke Whale
MARINE MAMMAL	NOFS	Northern Fur Seal
MARINE MAMMAL	SEOT	Sea Otter
MARINE MAMMAL	STSL	Stellar's Sea Lion
MARINE MAMMAL	UNWH	Unidentified Whale
OTHER	BLBE	Black Bear
OTHER	BRBE	Brown Bear
OTHER	GRWO	Grey Wolf
OTHER	MOGO	Mountain Goat
OTHER	MOOS	Moose
OTHER	RIOT	River Otter
PHALAROPE	REPH	Red Phalarope
PHALAROPE	RNPH	Red-necked Phalarope
PHALAROPE	UNPH	Unidentified Phalarope
RAPTOR	BAEA	Bald Eagle
RAPTOR	GOEA	Golden Eagle
RAPTOR	UNEA	Unidentified Eagle
RAPTOR	UNRA	Unidentified Raptor
SHOREBIRD	BLOY	Black Oystercatcher
SHOREBIRD	BLTU	Black Turnstone
SHOREBIRD	GBHE	Great Blue Heron
SHOREBIRD	LEYE	Lesser Yellowlegs
SHOREBIRD	SEPL	Semipalmated Plover
SHOREBIRD	SPSA	Spotted Sandpiper
SHOREBIRD	SURF	Surfbird
SHOREBIRD	UNSB	Unidentified Shorebird
SHOREBIRD	WHIM	Whimbrel
TERN	ALTE	Aleutian Tern
TERN	ARTE	Arctic Tern

GROUP	ABBREVIATION	SPECIES
TERN	CATE	Caspian Tern
TERN	UNTE	Unidentified Tern
TERRESTRIAL BIRD	AMRO	American Robin
TERRESTRIAL BIRD	BASW	Barn Swallow
TERRESTRIAL BIRD	BBMA	Black-billed Magpie
TERRESTRIAL BIRD	BEKI	Belted Kingfisher
TERRESTRIAL BIRD	CLSW	Cliff Swallow
TERRESTRIAL BIRD	CORA	Common Raven
TERRESTRIAL BIRD	NOCR	Northwestern Crow
TERRESTRIAL BIRD	RUHU	Rufous Hummingbird
TERRESTRIAL BIRD	UNSW	Unidentified Swallow
TERRESTRIAL BIRD	VGSW	Violet-Green Swallow
TERRESTRIAL BIRD	WSOW	Western Screech Owl
TUBENOSE	BFAL	Black-footed Albatross
TUBENOSE	FTSP	Fork-tailed Storm Petrel
TUBENOSE	LAAL	Laysan Albatross
TUBENOSE	LESP	Leach's Storm Petrel
TUBENOSE	MOPE	Mottled Petrel
TUBENOSE	NOFU	Northern Fulmar
TUBENOSE	SOSH	Sooty Shearwater
TUBENOSE	STAL	Short-tailed Albatross
TUBENOSE	STSH	Short-tailed Shearwater
TUBENOSE	UNAL	Unidentified Albatross
TUBENOSE	UNSH	Unidentified Shearwater
TUBENOSE	UNSP	Unidentified Storm Petrel

3.5.4 Number

The number of individuals in each group is recorded in the same field as the species. When birds or mammals become numerous or require identification, observers may request the vessel to slow to allow accurate identification and enumeration. If the observation is of a single individual there is no need to enter the number 1, as dLOG2 assigns the number 1 to all entries that do not include a number. Do not include more than one observation of the same individual or group. Birds that are flying above the survey vessel, or animals traveling along the transect in the same direction as the survey vessel provide examples where multiple counting should be avoided.

3.5.5 Behavior

The behavior field is used to record the habitat the individual or group is occupying at the time of the sighting (land, water or flying), prior to any disturbance response and includes observations of feeding while in any of those habitats (Table 5).

Table 5. Codes for behavior and habitat occupied for each sighting.

Habitat Occupied at Sighting (3 total)	Behavior/Activity Code and Description(6 total some may occur in more than one habitat type)
Air	Fly (Flying)
Land	Land (On land)
	Feed (Feeding)
Water	Wat/Fish (On water with fish)
	Fly/Fish (Flying with fish)
	Feed (Feeding)

3.5.6 Unique Situations

Each transect sampled is unique and a variety of situations will present themselves while conducting these surveys that can lead to methodological and interpretative questions. It is important to keep in mind the objective of these surveys when considering unique situations, namely to provide accurate estimates of the species composition, density, abundance and population trends of species of marine birds and mammals over time. Repeatability is a critical assumption in the interpretation of the data collected, and includes correct identifications, accurate delineation of the sampling window dimensions (e.g. transect width, length and height), and accurate counts of individuals. Following are a few examples of commonly encountered situations and how they can be resolved, excerpted from Appendix B.

1.   Sampling Window - spatial

The purpose of the survey is to count birds and otters, and many observers feel compelled to record *every* bird and otter they see, disregarding the boundaries of the sampling window. Exercise discipline, and avoid extending the sampling window to include sightings. If in doubt, ask the driver or other observer for their opinion. It seems rather obvious, but once and for all: *If a bird or otter is not within the sampling window, do not record it!* (Just say NO).

2.   Sampling Window - temporal

The ideal way to conduct a census or survey of animal populations would be to take a snapshot of the entire study area at a single point in time. This would allow you to count every animal present within the study area and eliminate the possibility of double-counting individuals. Obviously this is presently impossible, so an approximation of this method is required. The solution is to sample a survey "window" that is moving through space and time. In order to approximate the instantaneous nature of a snapshot, the window would ideally be sampled for a split-second, then the boat would move on. Again, this is not practical, and is approximated by moving the boat along the transect at a relatively constant velocity. Problems arise when the boat comes to a stop. This can happen for a variety of reasons: mechanical problems, difficult species identifications, counting large groups of birds at colonies, etc. For the purposes of this study, *if the boat has stopped moving for any reason, the sampling window is closed until you resume surveying.*

To fully understand this concept, imagine you are stopped at a salmon stream to count a large group of gulls. If you are stopped for one minute and count fly-throughs, you introduce a slight positive bias to your count for the transect. However, if you sit at the stream for an hour and count fly-throughs, you introduce a larger bias to your count. As in section III.C.1. above, the purpose of the survey is not to record every single bird and mammal that you see, but rather to conduct a statistically valid sample of these animals within the study area.

3.   Rocks

Animals located on rocks are recorded as animals on land. A problem arises when a rock is located more than 100m from the shoreline. A general rule of thumb is: if the rock appears to be exposed at mean high water (MHW), consider it as shoreline, and record the sighting as "side 1." Small islands fit this description well. If the rock appears to be covered at high water, record the sighting on the right side of the data sheet. This situation gives rise to the seemingly cryptic description of an animal located greater than 100m from shore, on land.

4.   Ice

Bearing in mind that ice represents both a hazard and an obstacle, there are a few comments about ice located within transects. The first is a general rule of thumb put forth by Greg Balogh: *if an iceberg is large enough that you would rather not have it dropped on your head, then don't hit it with the boat.* The second point deals with ice that obstructs survey of the transect. If ice prevents your ability to adequately see portions of the transect, estimate the percentage of the transect area that cannot be surveyed and record this value in the comments section of the data sheet. Remember to draw a picture of the ice coverage on the back of the data sheet. The estimate of the area that cannot be surveyed and a map can be used to calculate a correction factor for the unsurveyed habitat.

*** If ice prevents the boat from traveling part of the transect course BUT you can still scan the actual transect line with reasonable accuracy, record sightings as if the boat were on the actual transect track. Make a note on the header sheet (Transect log) whenever this procedure is necessary.

5.   Flushing and Diving

The question of animals that flush or dive ahead of the boat comes down to a single point: did that activity of the survey vessel cause the animal to alter its behavior? If so, then record the animal(s) on the data sheet. The only rule is to use good judgment and common sense. Bald eagles (BAEA) are not nailed to trees; they come and go of their own free will. If an eagle sighted in a tree several hundred meters ahead of the boat takes flight, do not automatically assume that your boat was the cause. He may have just gone off to feed. This is a subjective decision on the part of the individual observer. Feel free to discuss the situation with the other crew members. The final call should go to the observer who made the sighting in the first place.

6.   Rollup

A special case of flushing is known as rollup. This occurs when birds flushed by the survey vessel fly ahead and land farther along in the transect. These animals could then be counted multiple times, depending on their behavior and the length of the transect. Again, use common sense. If a flock of 12 harlequin ducks (HADU) flush forward into the transect, and immediately around the next bend you sight "another" flock of 12 HADUs, consider the possibility that they are the same flock.

An additional confounding situation would be if in the example presented above, the second flock contained 17 HADUs. At least 5 more HADUs are present on the transect than were seen previously. This situation could be recorded as a new sighting of 17 HADUs (when for example another group of 12 is nearby), or the original 12 *plus* an additional sighting of 5.

7.   Species Identification

Several assumptions should be avoided while identifying an animal to species.

The first is when you can ID a bird to the level of genus perhaps (murrelet, murre, cormorant, etc.) but not to species. Avoid saying: it was a murre, and since common murres are more abundant in Prince William Sound than thick-billed murres, it must have been a common murre. *If you aren't sure*, then record it as an unknown murre. Assuming the species based on relative abundance may only serve to perpetuate the illusion that one species is more abundant than the other. The most common occurrence of this is with marbled murrelets (MAMU) and Kittlitz's murrelet (KIMU). If you do not see adequate field marks, do not assume it is a MAMU. Record it as an identified murrelet of the genus *Brachyramphus* (BRMU).

The second situation occurs when mixed flocks are counted. If there are 25 gulls on a rock, and 22 of them are positively identified as mew gulls (MEGU), but the remaining 3 gulls are obscured so no field marks can be seen, do not assume them to be MEGUs. Record those 3 as unidentified gulls (UNGU). If you aren't satisfied with that identification, then maneuver the boat for a better view so you can see field marks. The exception to this rule is for waterfowl. Often, hens are difficult to identify to species. However, if a flock of hens and drakes are sighted, it is relatively safe to count them all as the same species.

8.   Distance Inland

The primary objective of this survey is not to record terrestrial animals. However, non-target species that are sighted should be recorded. Do not record sightings of animals that are greater than 100 m inland from the shoreline. This includes birds located far upstream, or bald eagles

(BAEA) soaring or perched in trees well inland. If you make a really spectacular sighting of a terrestrial mammal that doesn't belong on the data sheet and feel you have to tell someone about it, record it in the comments section.

3.6 Post-collection Processing of Data
After each field day, the following tasks are to be completed:

- Field personnel are to review data logs and edit dLOG2 as necessary to ensure legibility and resolve any discrepancies in data entry.
- Make identifications (if possible) of any taxa for which field identifications were in question and revise taxa names on data logs and in DLOG2 accordingly.
- Review dLOG2 data entries for the day to verify data entry. Record all edits of electronic data files in dLOG2.
- Download files from data collection computers and digital cameras. Store these and provide additional documentation as needed.
- Make a backup copy (cd or other removable media) of all data collected.
- Check and charge and replace batteries in electronic equipment as needed.
- Provide a summary of activities and observations for the day including any problems, suggestions for modifications in procedures, and unusual occurrences or observations.
- Prepare field transect log sheets and equipment for the following day's use.
- Review transect checklist for the following days anticipated survey work.

After each field trip or cruise, the following are to be completed:

-Produce a summary of the cruise based on summaries of daily activities and observations
-

3.7 End-of-season Procedures
At the end of each field season all equipment should be cleaned, serviced, and batteries removed for storage. Optics, and other equipment and field gear should be assessed for repair or replacement needs. Skiff and engines should be winterized and prepared for seasonal storage.

After each field season, the following are to be done:

- Clean and check all mechanical and electronic equipment and field gear for needed repair and store appropriately.
- Make repairs or obtain replacements for damaged or lost equipment or supplies.
- Produce a field season summary report based on daily sampling reports. This should be completed within on week of completion of the seasons.

4 Data Handling, Analysis and Reporting

4.1 Metadata Procedures

See SWAN Nearshore Protocol Narrative Section 4.0 (Dean and Bodkin 2011). The marine bird and mammal survey procedure is designed to meet the following objectives. One is to estimate the species composition and density of marine birds and mammals along systematically located transects within SWAN Parks and regions in the Gulf of Alaska. A second objective is to estimate population sizes and associated variances of selected marine birds and mammals within SWAN Parks and regions. The third objective is to detect trends in abundance of marine bird and mammal populations over time SWAN parks and regions.

4.2 Overview of Database Design

Currently, data is stored in GIS files and/or flat files. A database will be developed once several years of data are collected and best methods for entry, checking, storing, analyzing and reporting are finalized.

4.3 Data Entry, Verification and Editing

Data currently is downloaded into a GIS software package for editing and analysis. Data is edited as soon as possible upon returning from the field. Raw data files are backed-up. The project manager edits data to correct discrepancies.

4.4 Routine Data Summaries and Statistical Analyses

The overall analytical approach is described in the SWAN Protocol Narrative (Dean and Bodkin 2011) that relies on data collected from most sampling protocols. In preparation of providing data derived from these surveys, annual summaries should be completed. Annual analyses should consist of mapping the distribution and estimating the density, abundance, and standard error of the estimates for each of the marine birds and mammals encountered during the winter and summer marine bird surveys. Following 5 years of data collection a spatial analysis should be conducted to explore relations between density and abundance, by species, and physical and biological attributes of the environment. Annual reporting of marine bird surveys should consist of maps of the distribution of each species for winter and summer surveys (Figure 1-2) and summary tables of the densities (se) of each species (Table 7). The following outline describes these analyses.

0

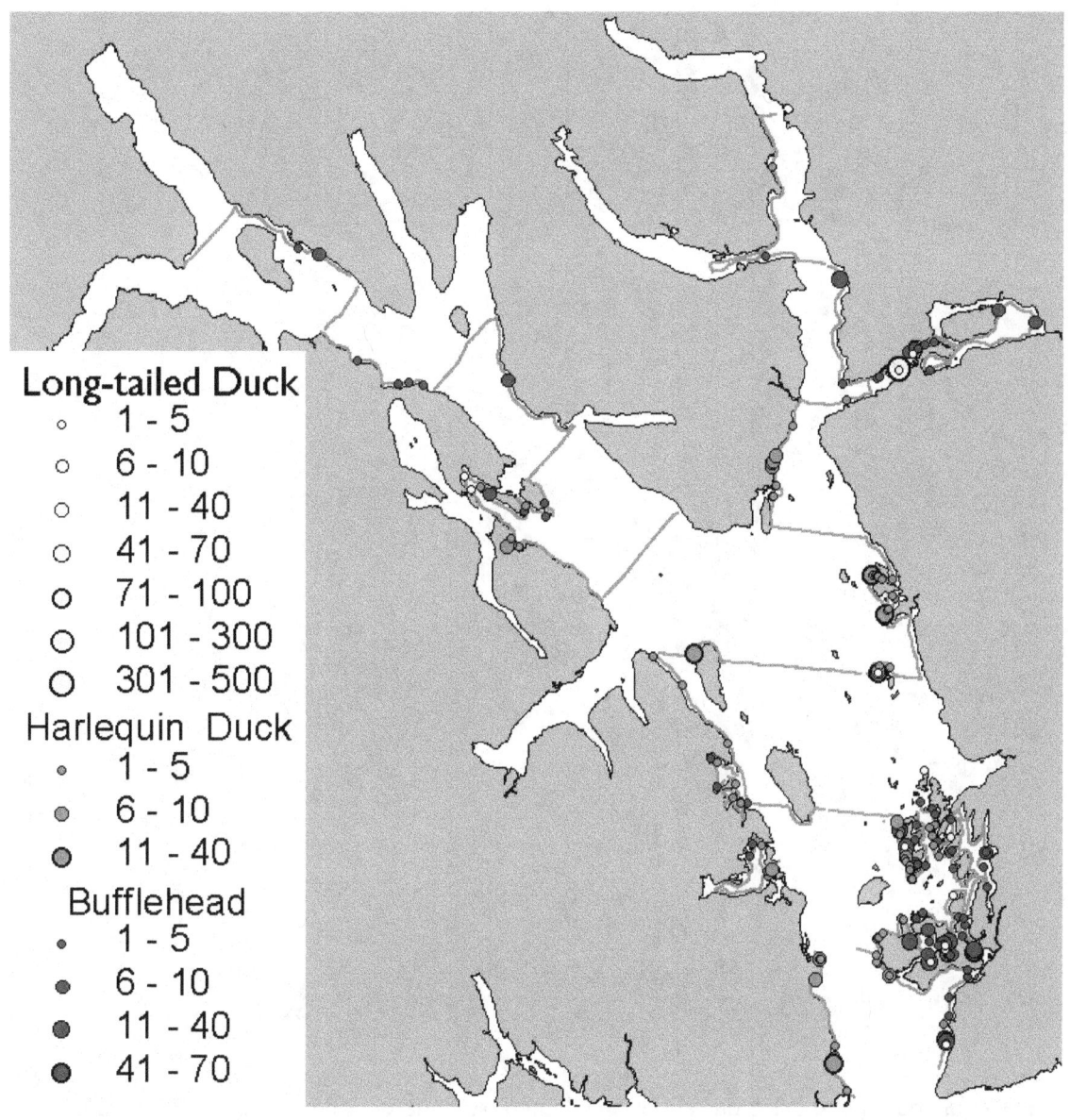

Long-tailed Duck
- ∘ 1 - 5
- ∘ 6 - 10
- ∘ 11 - 40
- ∘ 41 - 70
- ○ 71 - 100
- ○ 101 - 300
- ○ 301 - 500

Harlequin Duck
- · 1 - 5
- • 6 - 10
- • 11 - 40

Bufflehead
- · 1 - 5
- • 6 - 10
- • 11 - 40
- • 41 - 70

Figure 1. Harlequin duck, long-tailed duck (formerly named old-squaws), and bufflehead observations in March 2001 in Glacier Bay NP. Gray lines are the survey track lines.

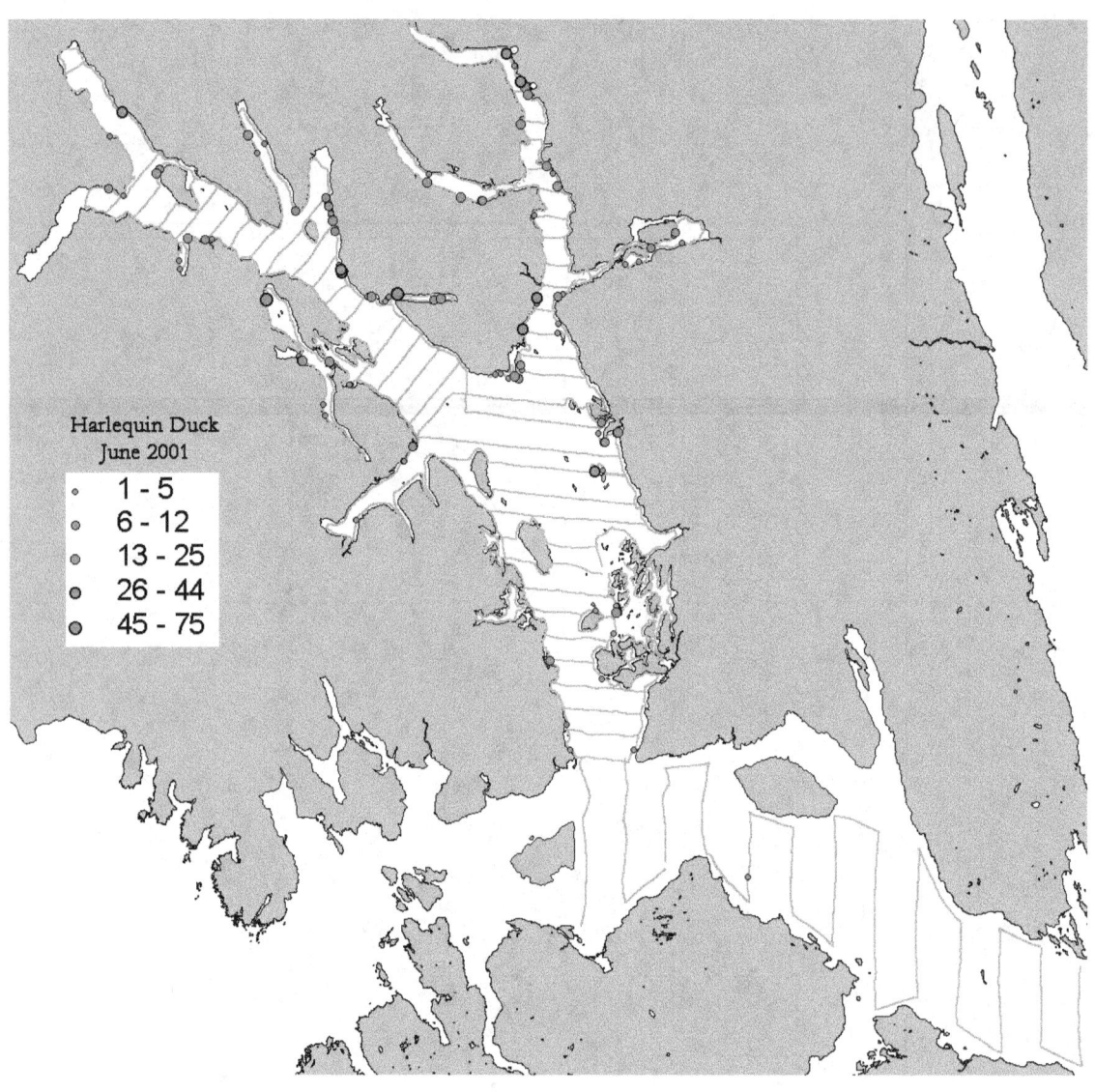

Figure 2. Harlequin duck, long-tailed duck (formerly named old-squaws), and bufflehead observations in June 2001, in Glacier Bay NP. Gray lines are the survey track lines.

Table 6. Example of a summary of the species composition, number, proportion and density of marine birds and mammals encountered during nearshore marine birds and mammals survey in Glacier Bay National Park

Table 6. Species observed during the 2001 nearshore marine birds and mammals survey in Glacier Bay National Park and Preserve (GBNPP). Code is the abbreviation appearing in the raw data files (W: waterfowl; S: seabirds; B: shorebirds and O: other). Name is the common name. Number counted, percentage of all birds (or % of marine mammals or % of other mammals), and density (#/km^2) are given. Several subtotals are also presented to allow comparison with previous reports. No off-transect sightings are included in these numbers.

Code	Name	March #	March %	March Density	June #	June %	June Density	June:Mar #	June:Mar Density
COLO	Common Loon (W)	15	0.09	0.15	45	0.10	0.16	3.00	1.06
PALO	Pacific Loon (W)	15	0.09	0.15	45	0.10	0.16	3.00	1.06
RTLO	Red-throated Loon (W)	0	0.00	0.00	21	0.05	0.07	.	.
YBLO	Yellow-billed Loon (W)	1	0.01	0.01	3	0.01	0.01	3.00	1.06
UNLO	Unidentified Loon (W)	9	0.05	0.09	50	0.11	0.17	5.56	1.96
	All Loons	**40**	**0.23**	**0.39**	**164**	**0.37**	**0.57**	**4.10**	**1.44**
HOGR	Horned Grebe (W)	154	0.89	1.51	0	0.00	0.00	0.00	0.00
RNGR	Red-necked Grebe (W)	3	0.02	0.03	0	0.00	0.00	0.00	0.00
UNGR	Unknown Grebe (W)	18	0.10	0.18	1	0.00	0.00	0.06	0.02
FTSP	Fork-tailed Storm-Petrel (S)	3	0.02	0.03	3	0.01	0.01	1.00	0.35
PECO	Pelagic Cormorant (S)	187	1.08	1.84	69	0.16	0.24	0.37	0.13
GBGH	Great Blue Heron (B)	7	0.04	0.07	10	0.02	0.03	1.43	0.50
CAGO	Canada Goose (W)	177	1.02	1.74	551	1.24	1.91	3.11	1.10
BRAN	Brant (W)	0	0.00	0.00	4	0.01	0.01	.	.
MALL	Mallard (W)	771	4.46	7.58	304	0.68	1.05	0.39	0.14
GADW	Gadwall (W)	0	0.00	0.00	2	0.00	0.01	.	.
GWTE	Green-winged Teal (W)	0	0.00	0.00	3	0.01	0.01	.	.
AMWI	American Wigeon (W)	16	0.09	0.16	95	0.21	0.33	5.94	2.09
NOPI	Northern Pintail (W)	2	0.01	0.02	0	0.00	0.00	0.00	0.00
NOSH	Northern Shoveler (W)	0	0.00	0.00	2	0.00	0.01	.	.
GRSC	Greater Scaup (W)	0	0.00	0.00	10	0.02	0.03	.	.
SCAU	Unidentified Scaup (W)	145	0.84	1.43	30	0.07	0.10	0.21	0.07
BLSC	Black Scoter (W)	204	1.18	2.01	10	0.02	0.03	0.05	0.02
SUSC	Surf Scoter (W)	1706	9.88	16.78	6949	15.64	24.05	4.07	1.43
WWSC	White-winged Scoter (W)	824	4.77	8.10	7132	16.06	24.69	8.66	3.05
UNSC	Unidentified Scoter (W)	172	1.00	1.69	3350	7.54	11.60	19.48	6.85
	All Scoter	**2906**	**16.82**	**28.58**	**17441**	**39.26**	**60.37**	**6.00**	**2.11**
HADU	Harlequin Duck (W)	394	2.28	3.88	1281	2.88	4.43	3.25	1.14
OLDS	Long-tailed Duck (W)	429	2.48	4.22	12	0.03	0.04	0.03	0.01
BAGO	Barrow's Goldeneye (W)	2706	15.67	26.62	39	0.09	0.13	0.01	0.01
COGO	Common Goldeneye (W)	134	0.78	1.32	0	0.00	0.00	0.00	0.00
UNGO	Unidentified Goldeneye (W)	1600	9.26	15.74	3	0.01	0.01	0.00	0.00
	All Goldeneye	**4440**	**25.70**	**43.67**	**42**	**0.09**	**0.15**	**0.01**	**0.00**
BUFF	Bufflehead (W)	594	3.44	5.84	0	0.00	0.00	0.00	0.00
RBME	Red-breasted Merganser (W)	495	2.87	4.87	17	0.04	0.06	0.03	0.01
COME	Common Merganser (W)	257	1.49	2.53	4192	9.44	14.51	16.31	5.74
UNME	Unidentified Merganser (W)	289	1.67	2.84	4	0.01	0.01	0.01	0.00
	All Merganser	**1041**	**6.03**	**10.24**	**4213**	**9.48**	**14.58**	**4.05**	**1.42**
UNDU	Unidentified Duck (W)	34	0.20	0.33	13	0.03	0.04	0.38	0.13
	All Ducks	**10772**	**62.36**	**105.95**	**23448**	**52.78**	**81.17**	**2.18**	**0.77**

Code	Name	March #	March %	March Density	June #	June %	June Density	June: Mar #	June:Mar Density
NOHA	Northern Harrier (O)	1	0.01	0.01	0	0.00	0.00	0.00	0.00
BAEA	Bald Eagle (O)	108	0.63	1.06	161	0.36	0.56	1.49	0.52
SEPL	Semipalmated Plover (B)	0	0.00	0.00	3	0.01	0.01	.	.
BLOY	Black Oystercatcher (B)	98	0.57	0.96	386	0.87	1.34	3.94	1.39
LEYE	Lesser Yellowlegs (B)	0	0.00	0.00	1	0.00	0.00	.	.
SPSA	Spotted Sandpiper (B)	0	0.00	0.00	1	0.00	0.00	.	.
WHIM	Whimbrel (B)	0	0.00	0.00	1	0.00	0.00	.	.
BLTU	Black Turnstone (B)	85	0.49	0.84	0	0.00	0.00	0.00	0.00
UNSB	Unidentified Shorebird (B)	15	0.09	0.15	6	0.01	0.02	0.40	0.14
PAJA	Parasitic Jaeger (S)	0	0.00	0.00	1	0.00	0.00	.	.
BLKI	Black-legged Kittiwake (S)	174	1.01	1.71	6027	13.57	20.86	34.64	12.19
BOGU	Bonaparte's Gull (S)	0	0.00	0.00	447	1.01	1.55	.	.
ROGU	Ross' Gull (S)	0	0.00	0.00	24	0.05	0.08	.	.
GWGU	Glaucous-winged Gull (S)	1906	11.03	18.75	2214	4.98	7.66	1.16	0.41
HEGU	Herring Gull (S)	21	0.12	0.21	114	0.26	0.39	5.43	1.91
MEGU	Mew Gull (S)	572	3.31	5.63	955	2.15	3.31	1.67	0.59
UNGU	Unidentified Gull (S)	419	2.43	4.12	456	1.03	1.58	1.09	0.38
	All Gull	**3092**	**17.90**	**30.41**	**10237**	**23.04**	**35.44**	**3.31**	**1.17**
ARTE	Arctic Tern (S)	0	0.00	0.00	952	2.14	3.30	.	.
COMU	Common Murre (S)	33	0.19	0.32	142	0.32	0.49	4.30	1.51
UNMU	Unidentified Murre (S)	0	0.00	0.00	1	0.00	0.00	.	.
PIGU	Pigeon Guillemot (S)	876	5.07	8.62	1863	4.19	6.45	2.13	0.75
KIMU	Kittlitz's Murrelet (S)	41	0.24	0.40	548	1.23	1.90	13.37	4.70
MAMU	Marbled Murrelet (S)	196	1.13	1.93	3312	7.46	11.46	16.90	5.95
BRMU	Brachyramphus Murrelet (S)	276	1.60	2.71	1777	4.00	6.15	6.44	2.27
	All Murrelet	**513**	**2.97**	**5.05**	**5637**	**12.69**	**19.51**	**10.99**	**3.87**
TUPU	Tufted Puffin (S)	0	0.00	0.00	23	0.05	0.08	.	.
	All Alcid	**1422**	**8.23**	**13.99**	**7666**	**17.26**	**26.54**	**5.39**	**1.90**
RUHU	Rufous Hummingbird (O)	0	0.00	0.00	1	0.00	0.00	.	.
BEKI	Belted Kingfisher (O)	0	0.00	0.00	4	0.01	0.01	.	.
BBMA	Black-billed Magpie (O)	58	0.34	0.57	0	0.00	0.00	0.00	0.00
NOCR	Northwestern Crow (O)	1018	5.89	10.01	687	1.55	2.38	0.67	0.24
CORA	Common Raven (O)	16	0.09	0.16	14	0.03	0.05	0.88	0.31
BASW	Barn Swallow (O)	0	0.00	0.00	21	0.05	0.07	.	.
VGSW	Violet-green Swallow (O)	0	0.00	0.00	1	0.00	0.00	.	.
UNSW	Unidentified Swallow (O)	0	0.00	0.00	13	0.03	0.04	.	.
AMRO	American Robin (O)	0	0.00	0.00	16	0.04	0.06	.	.
	All Seabirds (S)	**4704**	**27.23**	**46.27**	**18928**	**42.61**	**65.52**	**4.02**	**1.42**
	All Waterfowl (W)	**11164**	**64.63**	**109.81**	**24168**	**54.41**	**83.66**	**2.16**	**0.76**
	All Shorebirds (B)	**205**	**1.19**	**2.02**	**408**	**0.92**	**1.41**	**1.99**	**0.70**
	All Other Birds (O)	**1201**	**6.95**	**11.81**	**918**	**2.07**	**3.18**	**0.76**	**0.27**
	All Birds	**17274**	**100.00**	**169.90**	**44422**	**100.00**	**153.77**	**2.57**	**0.91**

Code	Name	March #	March %	March Density	June #	June %	June Density	June: Mar #	June:Mar Density
DAPO	Dall's porpoise	0	0.00	0.00	11	1.46	0.04	.	.
HAPO	Harbor Porpoise	80	23.19	0.79	69	9.16	0.24	0.86	0.30
HASE	Harbor Seal	80	23.19	0.79	366	48.61	1.27	4.58	1.61
STSL	Steller Sea Lion	92	26.67	0.90	53	7.04	0.18	0.58	0.20
SEOT	Sea Otter	93	26.96	0.91	231	30.68	0.80	2.48	0.87
HUWH	Humpback Whale	0	0.00	0.00	10	1.33	0.03	.	.
KIWH	Killer Whale	0	0.00	0.00	13	1.73	0.04	.	.
	All Marine Mammal	**345**		**3.39**	**753**		**2.61**	**2.18**	**0.77**

Code	Name	March #	March %	March Density	June #	June %	June Density	June: Mar #	June:Mar Density
BLBE	Black Bear	0	0.00	0.00	23	39.66	0.08	.	.
BRBE	Brown Bear	0	0.00	0.00	10	17.24	0.03	.	.
GRWO	Gray Wolf	0	0.00	0.00	3	5.17	0.01	.	.
MOGO	Mountain Goat	33	91.67	0.32	16	27.59	0.06	0.48	0.17
MOOS	Moose	3	8.33	0.03	3	5.17	0.01	1.00	0.35
RIOT	River Otter	0	0.00	0.00	3	5.17	0.01	.	.
	All Other	**36**		**0.35**	**58**		**0.20**	**1.61**	**0.57**

1) **Distribution**
   a. Species lists, by season, year and cumulative for marine birds and mammals
   b. Map distributions by season, year and cumulative for each species

2) **Density or Abundance**
   a. Calculate densities and population sizes by species and season

$$\hat{Y} = X \frac{\sum_{i=1}^{n} y_i}{\sum_{i=1}^{n} x_i}$$

Where:

$\hat{Y} =$ population estimate for a stratum.

$X =$ total area of the stratum

$y_i =$ number of birds counted on the ith transect

$x_i =$ area of ith transect

   b. Estimate variance in density and population size estimates

5

$$\hat{V}(\hat{Y}_R) = \frac{x_2}{\bar{x}^2} \cdot \frac{\sum y_i^2 + \hat{R}^2 \sum x_i^2 - 2\hat{R}^2 \sum x_i^2 - 2\hat{R} \sum x_i y_i}{n(n-1)}$$

Where:

$\hat{V}(\hat{Y}_R)$ = estimated variance of $\hat{Y}_R$

n = number of transects sampled in the stratum.

$\bar{x}$ = mean area of all transects sampled in the stratum.

$$\hat{R} = \frac{\sum_{i=1}^{n} y_i}{\sum_{i=1}^{n} x_i}$$

    c. Evaluate accuracy of density estimates (detection factors) by species
    d. Conduct sensitivity/power analyses by species and season after 5 years of data collection
    e. Tests of differences in marine bird and mammal densities among seasonal sampling periods and years will be by two-way analysis of variance
    f. Conduct trend analyses by species and season following 5 years of data collection

3) Spatial Analyses to be conducted following acquisition of 3-5 surveys
    a. Explore potential relations between species distribution and abundance by:
        i. Bathymetry
        ii. Substrate
        iii. Slope
        iv. Oceanography
        v. Weather
        vi. Proximity to Glaciers (latitude)
        vii. Prey densities (fish, benthic inverts, zooplankton, as available from other sources where required)
        viii. Freshwater input

Summary reports should be produced annually. Comprehensive reports should be produced after the first six years of sampling and at four year intervals following.

4.5 Report Format

Annual reports should include the summary tables described in 4.4 above. Also, reports should include plots of means of each metric of interest vs. time and vs. location. A process for determining what additional analyses may be appropriate for inclusion in comprehensive reports produced every four years and suggested formats for these are presented in the Protocol Narrative.

Reports will conform to specific guidelines set by the Natural Resource Publications Management website (http://www.nature.nps.gov/publications/NRPM/index.cfm). Reports will include maps, graphs, figures and other visuals to facilitate comprehension of findings.

4.6 Methods for Trend Analyses

Procedures for long-term trend analyses are presented in the SWAN Nearshore Protocol Narrative (Dean and Bodkin 2011).

4.7 Reporting Schedule

Summary reports should be produced annually. More comprehensive reports should be produced after the first five years of sampling and every four years thereafter.

5 Personnel Requirements and Training

5.1 Requirements and Training
Observers conducting surveys should be experienced and capable of identifying and enumerating all marine birds and mammals encountered in the course of these surveys. It is not necessary that the data recorder be able to identify birds and mammals but if they are it will allow breaks for the observers that could rotate duties between observer and recorder. At least one observer on each 3 person crew should have >10 days of experience as an observer conducting marine bird and mammal surveys in the north Pacific and will be recognized as a "lead" observer. Lead observers will provide instruction and approval of other observers to "lead" observer status. All personnel must be current with applicable safety training.

6 Operational Requirements and Workloads

6.1 Operational Requirements
Operational requirements include transportation and access to the each of the transects within each block, region and park, access and use of required optics, software and electronics (e.g. dLOG2, GPS), and access to taxonomic keys and guides to marine birds and mammals common to the Gulf of Alaska.

6.2 Annual Workload and Field Schedule
Workload includes 90 person days per year for field (30 for winter [2 crews of 3 for 5 days, one regions each winter]and 60 for summer for 2 regions [2 crews of 3 for 5 days, two regions each summer]) and 65 person days for office analysis and writing (15 per survey, and 20 for compilation among regions). Sampling is done from dedicated support vessels during the winter surveys. Summer sampling is conducted in conjunction with and supported with charters conducting invertebrate and algal sampling at intensive blocks as well as conducting sampling of other vital signs within the SWAN Nearshore Monitoring Program.

6.3 Facility and Equipment Needs
A charter vessel that accommodates six field crew members will be required. The vessel will be equipped or be able to accommodate two skiffs appropriate for surveying from. Three GPS units are required per each field trip as well as two ruggedized laptops with Dlog2 software loaded.

6.4 Start-up Costs and Budget Considerations
Startup costs include $2,000 for 4 copies of survey data entry software (DLOG2), $8,000 for 4 pair of binoculars (Leica, 10x 42 recommended) (4 additional pair available from sea otter foraging sampling), and $1,000 for miscellaneous field supplies such as field guides, clipboards, paper...). Annual operating budget estimated at approximately $27,300 for the winter surveys in 1 park, including $15,000 in vessel charter costs, $7,200 in salary costs, and $5,100 in travel related costs.

Costs for summer surveys are $39,200, reduced due to the costs of vessel charters being budgeted for under the invertebrate and algal sampling and reduced travel and supply costs.

7 Procedures for Revising the Protocol

All edits and amendments made to the protocol narrative and/or SOPs should be recorded in the revision history log table at the beginning of this document. Users of this protocol should promptly notify the project leader of the marine nearshore monitoring program of recommended edits or changes. The project leader will review and incorporate suggested changes as necessary, record these changes in the revision history log, and modify the date and version number on the title page of this document to reflect these changes.

It is anticipated that following at least five years of annual data collection it will be important to evaluate, in terms of power and sensitivity, the ability of the sampling design to detect change in the data derived from marine bird and mammals surveys. Following such analyses it may be appropriate to consider revising sampling design or data collection protocols.

8 Literature Cited

Armstrong, R. H. 1996. Guide to the Birds of Alaska.

Bodkin, J. L. and M. S. Udevitz. 1999. An aerial survey method to estimate sea otter abundance. *In* G. W. Garner, S. C. Amstrup, J. L. Laake, B. F. J. Manly, L. L. McDonald, and D. G. Robertson. Marine Mammal Survey and Assessment Methods. A.A. Balkema, Rotterdam.

Dahlmann, G., D. Timm, C. Averbeck, C. J. Camphuysen, H. Skov and J. Durinck. 1994. Oiled seabirds: comparative investigations on oiled seabirds and oiled beaches in The Netherlands, Denmark and Germany (1990-93). Marine Pollution Bulletin 28(5): 305-310.

Dean, T. A., and J. L. Bodkin. 2011. Protocol narrative for marine nearshore ecosystem monitoring in the Southwest Alaska Network of National Parks. Natural Resource Report NPS/SWAN/NRR—2011/XXX. National Park Service, Fort Collins, Colorado.

Draulans, D. 1982. Foraging and Size Selection of Mussels by the Tufted Duck, *Aythya Fuligula*. Journal of Animal Ecology 51(3): 943-956.

Esler, D., T. D. Bowman, K. A. Trust, B. E. Ballachey, T. A. Dean, S. C. Jewett, and C. O. O'Clair. 2002. Harlequin Duck Population Recovery Following the Exxon Valdez Oil Spill: Progress, Process, and Constraints. Marine Ecology Progress Series.

Esler, D., J. A. Schmutz, R. L. Jarvis and D. M. Mulcahy. 2000. Winter survival of adult female harlequin ducks in relation to history of contamination by the *Exxon Valdez* oil spill. Journal of Wildlife Management 64(3): 839-847.

Ford, G. 2004. Program Description and Users Manual *V* 2.1.4 R.G. Ford Consulting Co. dLOG2 software for biological Surveys: Data Entry and Real-time Mapping Program for Windows®. R.G. Ford Consulting Co., 2735 NE Weidler Street, Portland, OR.

Gould, P. J. and D. J. Forsell. 1989. Techniques for shipboard surveys of marine birds. Fish and Wildlife technical Report 25.

Hamilton, D., and T. Nudds. 2003. Effects of predation by common eiders (Somateria mollissima) in an intertidal rockweed bed relative to an adjacent mussel bed. Marine Biology 142(1): 1-12.

Irons, D. B., S. J. Kendall, W. P. Erickson, L. L. McDonald, and B. K. Lance. 2000. Nine Years after the Exxon Valdez Oil Spill: Effects on Marine Bird Populations in Prince William Sound, Alaska. The Condor 102: 723-737.

Irons, D. B., D. R. Nysewander and J. L. Trapp. 1988. Prince William Sound Sea Otter Distribution in Respect to Population Growth and Habitat Type. Prepared by Alaska

Investigations Field Office (Branch of Wetlands and Marine Ecology) and Wildlife Assistance (Marine Bird Project).

Lance, B. K., D. B. Irons, S. J. Kendall, and L. L. McDonald. 2001. An Evaluation of Marine Bird Population Trends Following the Exxon Valdez Oil Spill, Prince William Sound, Alaska. Marine Pollution Bulletin 42(4): 298-309.

Lindberg, D. R., J. A. Estes and K. I. Warheit. 1998. Human influences on trophic cascades along rocky shores. Ecological Applications 8(3): 880-890.

Marsh, C. P. 1986. Rocky Intertidal Community Organization: The Impact of Avian Predators on Mussel Recruitment. Ecology 67(3): 771-786.

Meire, P. M. 1993. The Impact of Bird Predation on Marine and Estuarine Bivalve Populations: A selective Review of Patterns and Underlying Causes Bivalve Filter Feeders in Estuarine and Coastal Ecosystem Processes. Springer-Verlag, Heidelberg, Germany, G 33.

Peterson, C. H., S. D. Rice, J. W. Short, D. Esler, J. L. Bodkin, B. E. Ballachey, and D. B. Irons. 2003. Long-term ecosystem response to the *Exxon Valdez* oil spill. Science 302: 2082-2086.

Sibley, D. A. 2000. The Sibley guide to birds. Alfred A. Knopf, Inc.

Trust, K. A., D. Esler, B. R. Woodin and J. J. Stegeman. 2000. Cytochrome P450 1A induction in sea ducks inhabiting nearshore areas of Prince William Sound, Alaska. Marine Pollution Bulletin 40(5): 397-403.

Udevitz, M. S., J. L. Bodkin, and D. P. Costa. 1995. Detection of Sea Otters in Boat-Based Surveys of Prince William Sound, Alaska. Marine Mammal Science. 11. (1.): 59-71.

West, Inc, Western EcoSystems Technology. 2003. Bootstrapping to investigate effects of sample size on variance and bias of estimated species totals for Prince William Sound Marine Bird Surveys.

Wynn, K. 1997. K. Wynn. Guide to Marine Mammals of Alaska. Alaska Sea Grant College Program, University of Alaska, Fairbanks

Yamamuro, M., N. Oka and J. Hiratsuka. 1998. Predation by diving ducks on the biofouling mussel *Musculista senhousia* in a eutrophic estuarine lagoon. Marine Ecology Progress Series 174: 101-106.

9 Appendices

9.1 Appendix A. Dlog2 Manual

dLOG2
Software for Biological Surveys

Data Entry and Real-time Mapping Program
for Windows®

Program Description
and
Users Manual
V 2.1.4

R.G. Ford Consulting Co.
2735 NE Weidler Street
Portland, OR 97232

(503) 287-5173
eci@teleport.com

September 2004

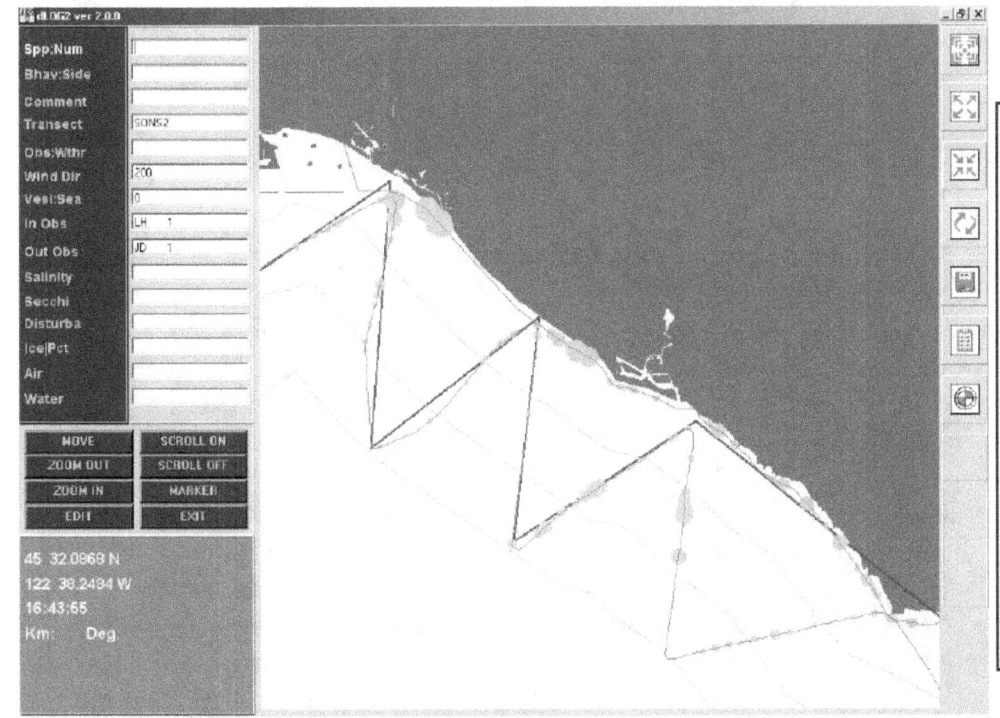

Sample dLog2 screen as seen during a data entry session. The red line shows the vessel track. Variably sized circles along the track show the positions of observations of bird flocks. Base map is derived from USGS or

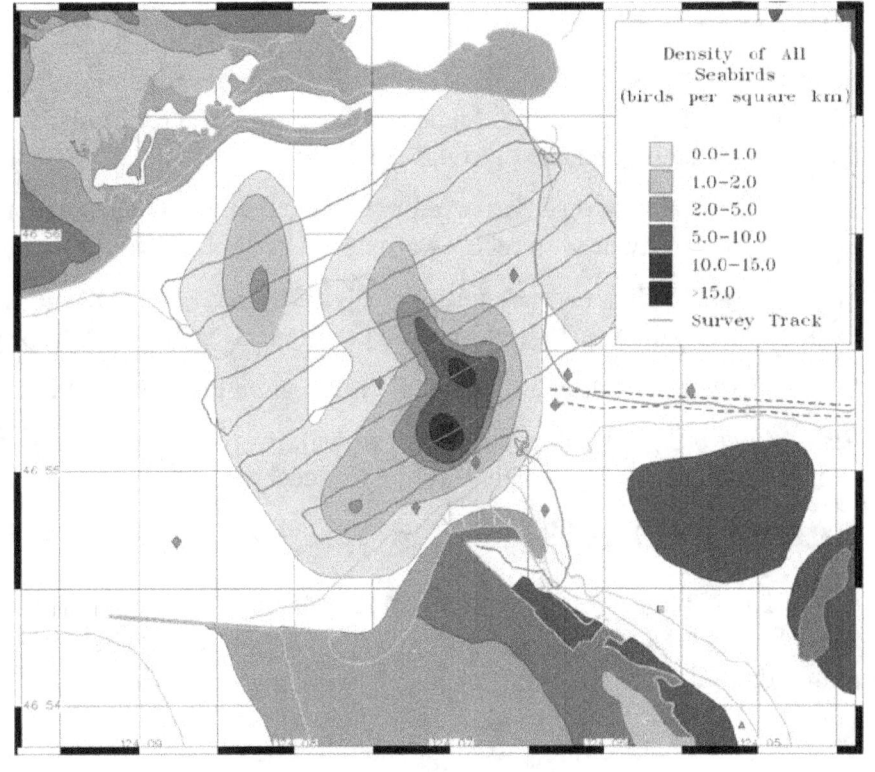

Density of All Seabirds
(birds per square km)

- 0.0–1.0
- 1.0–2.0
- 2.0–5.0
- 5.0–10.0
- 10.0–15.0
- >15.0
- Survey Track

Output from dLog2 data entry program that has been processed using a GIS to generate estimates of bird densities. The trackline of the vessel recording

dLOG2
Software for Biological Surveys

Data Entry and Real-time Mapping Program
for Windows®

Overview

dLOG2 is a data logging and real-time mapping program that plots trackline and data against a user defined basemap at the same time as the data are collected. The data entry procedure is user definable and is optimized to minimize the number of keystrokes required to enter each data record. Position data are read from a GPS unit connected to the host computer. Optionally, dLOG2 may be configured to accept input from an additional external device, such as a thermosalinigraph.

dLOG2 is designed for use on a wide variety of portable computers running Windows98 or higher. All data are written continuously to the hard disk in order to prevent information loss. It is also designed to be used with user-generated map backgrounds so that map data (ArcView Shape files) can be used to create functional background maps. The time required to become proficient with the program is quite short, typically requiring less than one half hour. Data files are written simultaneously in several common formats so that they may be easily imported into most commonly used software.

Installing dLOG2

dLOG2 is a Windows version of dLOG and should run on any Windows98, WindowsME, Windows2000, or WindowsXP machine. It requires a GPS with a serial connector. NOTE: If the GPS device is connected through a USB port, a serial to USB connector is required.)

Step 1: Double click on **Setup.exe** on the installation CD and accept all the defaults as it installs the files. You may need to reboot your computer one or more times.

Step 2: Double click on the appropriate **Jet40SP6.exe** file for your operating system (for example, for Windows2000 you would use **Jet40SP6_W2K.exe**). Again, accept any defaults.

Step 3: Create a **C:\dlog2** directory if your computer does not already have one.

Step 4 (optional): While you may run dLOG2 from the Start Menu, you might want to create a shortcut to dLOG2.exe and place it on your desktop.

Starting and Running dLOG2

dLOG2 may be initiated from the START Menu or from a shortcut on the Desktop. Sequentially, **dLOG2** will ask you to choose a map for the display and the path and name of the output data file.

First, you will be asked to choose the map for the display:

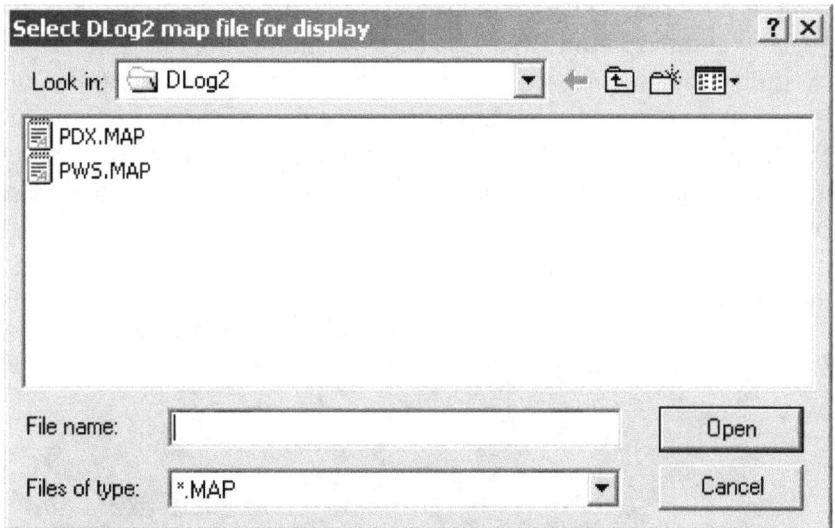

Choose a map from the list or navigate to another map. Note that several software programs use files with the extension .MAP, if a non-dLOG2 map file is chosen then an error will occur. Once the display map has been chosen, you will be asked to designate an output file.

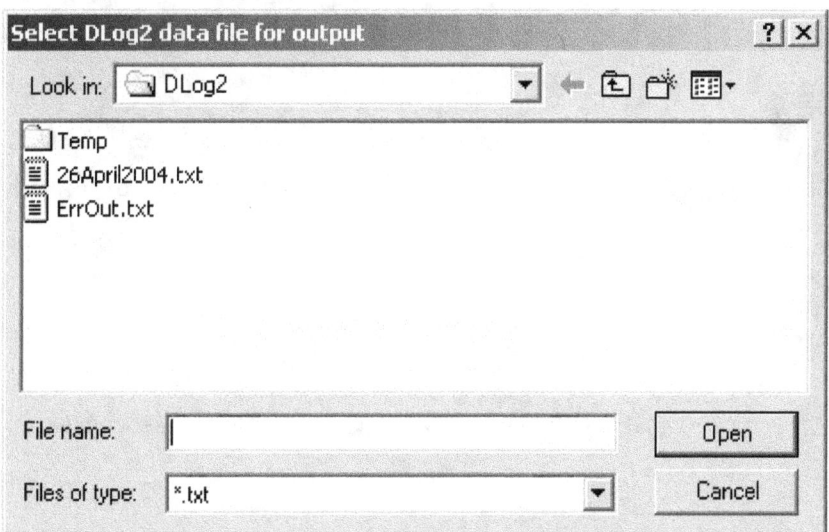

Choose an existing data file or type in the name of the data file where new data will be written. If you continue an existing file, non-volatile data fields will be filled using information on the last line of the existing data file. Files not created by **dLOG2** or damaged **dLOG2** data files will generate an error at this point.

dLOG2 Screen Areas

For speed and simplicity, **dLOG2** uses only one screen and accepts mostly keyboard input. The screen has five distinct areas: a map in a large portion of the screen, three data/menu blocks on the left side of the screen, and a column of icons on the right of the screen. The three blocks (from top to bottom) are for data entry, menu selection, and data display. Movement between the Data Editing Block and the Menu Block is accomplished using the [Esc] key. Executing a menu option or writing a data record occurs when the [Enter] key is pressed. Your current data entry field or menu option is indicated by highlighting, either of the field name in the Data Entry block, or the menu option in the menu block. Automated data acquisition occurs whether you are currently working in the Menu Block or in the Data Entry Block. Data acquired automatically are displayed in the Data Display Block. The icons provide alternative means of controlling the map display and setting the marker, as well as saving backup data files and capturing the screen to the clipboard.

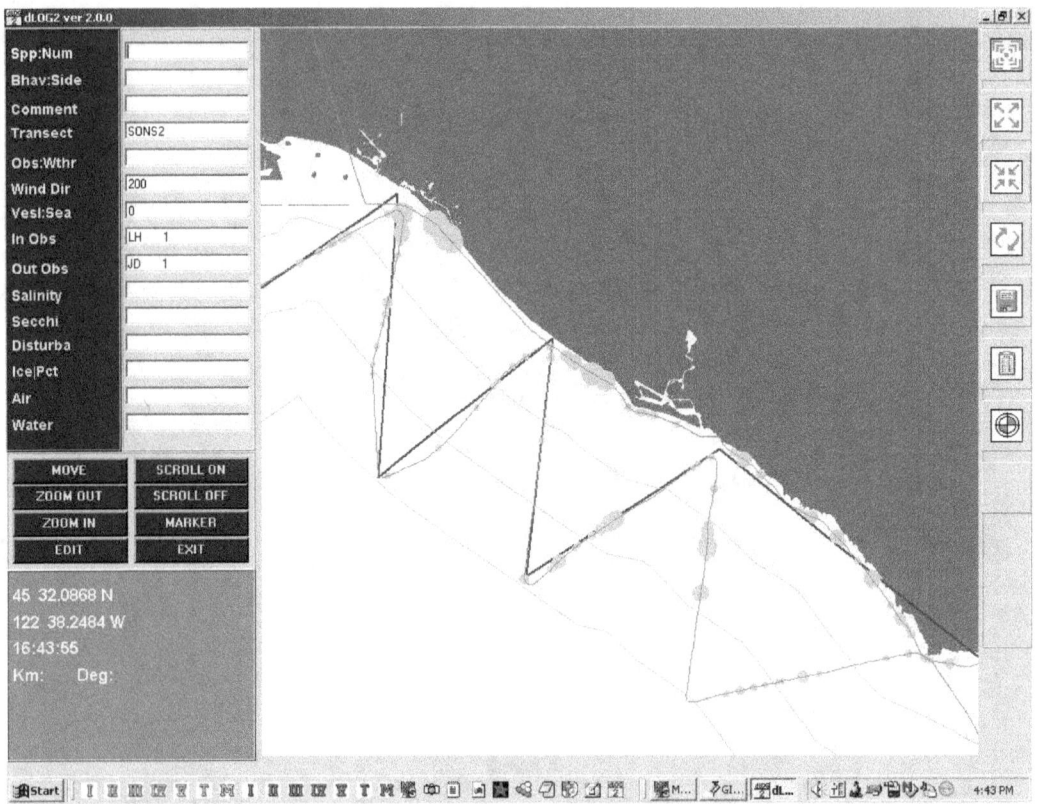

Data Entry Block

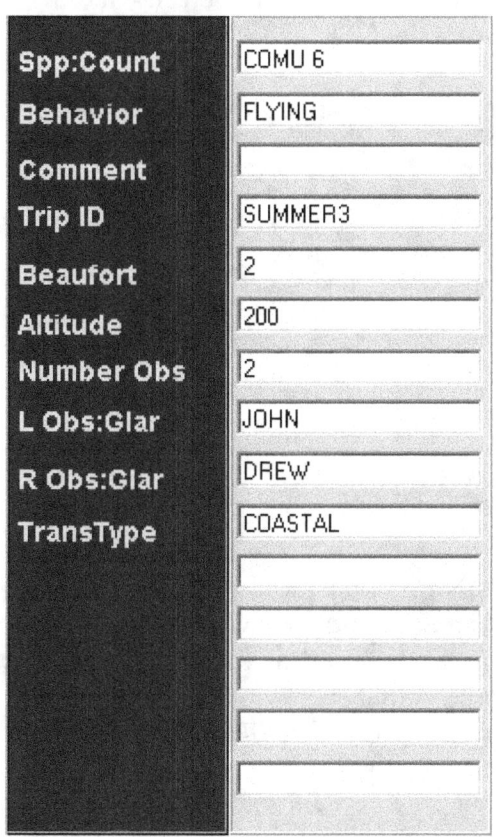

The **Data Entry Block** is used for entering new data. A data record is written when you are working in the Data Editing Block and you press [Enter]. You can tell when you are working in the Data Entry Block because one of the fields will be highlighted and will contain a blinking cursor. Pressing [Enter] will cause a record containing all the data fields to be written to disk and stamped with the time and position for the instant that the [Enter] key was pressed. Movement between data entry fields is accomplished using the up or down arrow keys (left and right arrows do not work). Movement between the Data Entry Block and the Menu Block is accomplished using the [Esc] key. Pressing [Esc] does not cause a data record to be written. The block consists of up to 15 data entry fields, each up to 10 characters in length, and each with the following user definable attributes (Defined in FIELDS.DAT -- see **Configuration of dLOG2** below):

Menu Block

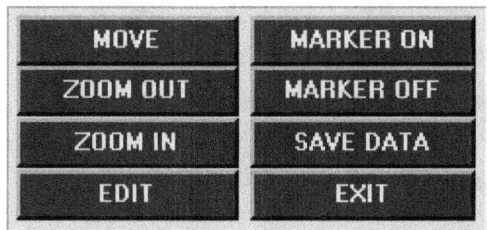

The **Menu Block** executes commands for controlling the map window, editing data records, setting the on-screen marker, and exiting **dLOG2**. Movement between the Data Entry Block and the Menu Block is controlled by the [Esc] key. When the Menu Block is in use, one of the menu options will be highlighted. When the Data Entry Block is in use, one of the data entry fields will be high-lighted. For both blocks, [Esc] will place you at the top of the block. Within the Menu Block, move between options using the up or down arrow keys. Activate the currently highlighted option by pressing [Enter].

Move   Causes the map window to be recentered on the current position. Normally, this will be the last position read from the GPS.

19

| Zoom Out | Causes the map window to increase the area mapped by a factor of 2 so that four times as much area is shown in the map window. The screen will be recentered on the last position read from the GPS. |

Zoom Out Causes the map window to increase the area mapped by a factor of 2 so that four times as much area is shown in the map window. The screen will be recentered on the last position read from the GPS.

Zoom In Causes the map window to decrease the area mapped by a factor of 0.5 so that 1/4 as much area is shown in the map window. The screen will be recentered on the last position read from the GPS.

Edit Enables editing of the user entered records. After editing, choose OK to

	RecNum	Spp:Cnt	Behavior	Plumage	Distance	Depth	Comment	Trip ID	Beaufort	Swell Ht	Number Obs	L Obs/Glar	R Obs/Glar
1	2	MAMU 1						WATSON-13	1	2	1	JAN	2
2	3	MAMU 1						WATSON-13	1	2	1	JAN	2
3	4	COMU 1						WATSON-13	1	2	1	JAN	2
4	5	COMU 1	FLY					WATSON-13	1	2	1	JAN	2
5	7	GULL 1						WATSON-13	1	2	1	JAN	2
6	8	GULL 9						WATSON-13	1	2	1	JAN	2
7	9	M 1						WATSON-13	2	4	1	JAN	2
8	10	M 1						WATSON-13	2	4	1	JAN	2
9	11	K 1						WATSON-13	2	4	1	JAN	2
10	12	COMU 7						WATSON-13	2	4	1	JAN	2
11	13	COMU 8						WATSON-13	2	4	1	JAN	2

(Search / Delete Row / OK / Cancel buttons; field: Spp:Cnt =)

accept edits and return to the main screen, or CANCEL to abandon edits and return to the main screen.

Marker On Positions an on-screen marker at your current position. After the marker has been set, the fourth line of the Data Display Block will show the heading and distance between the current position and the marker position. This information is also recorded in the output file. This functionality is equivalent to the 'Man Overboard' function on most GPS units. To remove the marker, select Marker Off.

Marker Off Removes the Marker display from the screen and discontinues heading and distance recording.

Save Data Creates a numbered backup of the data file in the location specified in GPS.DAT. For example, if the basic data file is called **outputfile.txt**. the backup will be **outputfile1.txt** or **outputfile2.txt**. Choosing this option once will create **outputfile1.txt**, choosing it twice will create **outputfile2.txt**, choosing it a third time will overwrite **outputfile1.txt**, etc.

Exit Ends the **dLOG2** session and saves four sets of data files. The basic **dLOG2** output file, which has been saved frequently during the session, is saved once again. Three additional output files derived from this file are saved when the session is ended: (1) an Excel file version of the basic data, (2) an ArcView Shape file version of the user-generated records (observation data), and (3) an ArcView Shape file version of the trackline. The file names are created by **dLOG2** from the file name used for the basic data file, and are placed in the same location as the basic data file.

Data Display Block

```
45 32.071 N

122 38.242 W

11:33:34

Mark Km: 8.449 Deg: 66

Record: 20
```

The ***Data Display Block*** shows a readout of automatically acquired data related to the current position. There are five lines that display the following data:

(1) Latitude (degrees, minutes)
(2) Longitude (degrees, minutes)
(3) Time (hour, minute, second)
(4) Distance and Angle to Current Position of Marker
(5) Record Number (this corresponds to the row number in the output files)

All data fields except the time (3) are updated following acquisition of a valid GPS position. If **dLOG2** cannot obtain a valid position, asterisks will show to the right of the latitude and longitude values. Time is updated every second.

Icons

Zoom to extent of map
Redraws the screen so that the entire area of the map is displayed.

Zoom Out
Redraws the screen so that more area is visible (identical to Zoom Out in the Menu Block).

Zoom In to left button click
Creates a red cursor which may be placed anywhere on the map display. A left button click will cause the display to be redraw with a more detailed view centered there.

Refresh map
Redraws the display without changing the view.

Back Up All Data
Creates a backup of the data file in the location specified in GPS.DAT. If the basic data file is called **outputfile.txt**. the backup will be **outputfile1.txt** or **outputfile2.txt**

Copy Map to Clipboard
Copies the map display to the clipboard. It can then be pasted into a document or saved as a graphic file.

Set Distance/Angle Marker
Creates a marker cursor which may be placed anywhere on the map display. A left button click will set the marker. Line Four of the Data Display Block will indicate the distance and angle from your current GPS position to this marker. A right button click removes the marker.

Automatic Configuration of dLOG2: dLOGSetup

Input data for **dLOG2** is contained in several external files. These files may be modified manually by using a simple text editor such as Notepad (see below for instructions for manual configuration).   An automatic configuration program, **dLOGSetup**, is under development, and includes a facility for creating or modifying the FIELDS.DAT, ALIAS.DAT and HOTKEY.DAT files, as well as specifying the components of the on-screen map and configuring the GPS. A preliminary version of **dLOGSetup** is included in the installation; the first three options are operational in this version.

Manual Configuration of dLOG2

Data Entry Fields

The definition of the data entry fields are user definable based on information provided in the FIELDS.DAT file in the **C:\Program Files\dLOG2** directory. The FIELDS.DAT file may be created or modified using a simple text editor such as NOTEPAD.

Columns 1-10   Field Name: Mnemonic title that appears to the left of each data entry field in the Data Entry Block.

Columns 11-15   Field type, right justified. 1 is integer, 2 is real, and 3 is text. Mixed fields are defined as text.

Columns 16-20   Whether or not field is mixed. 1 is mixed, 0 is normal. Mixed fields are for rapid entry of a code and a count. The field is automatically separated into a 5 character alphameric sequence and a 5 character integer. Thus, the hurried entry "14MAMU" or "MA14MU" are automatically processed to be "MAMU14". The default integer value is 1. The entry "MAMU" is automatically processed to be "MAMU1".

Columns 21-25   Whether or not field is reset after each data record is written. 0 is reset after writing record (volatile field), 1 is retain data until data are modified (persistent field).

Columns 26-30   Automatic display flag. Not used in dLOG2.

Columns 31-35   Number of decimal places. This affects only the output and display of real (type 2) numbers.

Hot Keys

To speed up data entry, you can define the function keys on your keyboard to place a particular data string into a particular field. The definitions of the hotkeys are contained in the file HOTKEY.DAT in the **C:\PROGRAM FILES\dLOG2** directory. The first field is the function key number, the second field is data entry field number (where field one is at the top of the screen), and the third field is the data string. Fields in the HOTKEY.DAT file are blank delimited. The data entry string must be single quote delimited. For example, the entries:

$$1 \quad 2 \quad \text{'FLYING'}$$
$$2 \quad 2 \quad \text{'SITTING'}$$
$$3 \quad 3 \quad \text{'FISH VSL'}$$

would place the string "FLYING" in field 2 (second from the top) when the F1 key was pressed as long as you were working in the Data Entry Block. You would not need to key down to field 2 and type in the word "FLYING". Similarly pressing the F2 key would place the string "SITTING" in field 2. Pressing F3 would cause "FISH VSL" to be written to data entry field 3. The HOTKEY.DAT file may be created or modified using a simple text editor such as NOTEPAD.

Aliases

Aliases are text strings that replace other text strings within a given field. For example, if the string "C" were aliased to "COMU" in field 1, then entering "C" would cause "COMU" to be written to the output file. Entering a "C" embedded in another string such as "COLO" would have no effect, nor would entering "C" in any other field. Aliases are defined in the file **C:\PROGRAM FILES\DLOG2\ALIAS.DAT**. Format is column delimited. Columns 1-5 left justified is the field number. Columns 6-15 left justified is the original string. Columns 21-30 left justified is the replacement string. The entries:

$$1 \quad \text{C} \qquad \text{COMU}$$
$$1 \quad \text{L} \qquad \text{COLO}$$

in the ALIAS.DAT file would cause "C" to be replaced with "COMU" and "L" to be replaced with "COLO" in User Field 1. The ALIAS.DAT file may be created or modified using a simple text editor such as NOTEPAD.

Map Creation

dLOG2 displays a background map constructed of Arc View Shape files in geographic coordinates (latitude/longitude). The colors for the display are determined by entries in the .MAP file. This is an ASCII text file describing the shape files to be used. The format of the file is simple and can be edited using NOTEPAD. Here is an example file. The file must have the extension .MAP.

```
'pwspol2.shp'    'DEEPBATH'
'pwspol1.shp'
'SHALLOWBATH'
'pwsland.shp'    'LAND'
'pwsbath2.shp'   'DEEPBATH'
```

The first part of each line (including obligatory single quote marks) describes the path and name of each Shape file; the second part describes the display desired. Colors are determined according to the following convention: LAND is green polygons, DEEPBATH is dark blue polygons or lines, SHALLOWBATH is light blue polygons or lines, HEXAGON is light green points, REGISTER is blue and white points, and SURVEY is purple lines.

Configuring the GPS

The GPS is configured using the file GPS.DAT, which may be created or modified using a simple text editor such as NOTEPAD.

Line 1 sets the serial port that **dLOG2** reads. A typical line would read

```
COM1,4800,N,8,
```

Which describes the GPS settings (port, baud rate, parity, data bytes, stop bit).

Line 2 sets the time interval between fixes, in hundredths of seconds. A typical line would read

```
150
```

An interval of 5 to 10 seconds (500 or 1000) works well in light aircraft or helicopters moving at about 100 kt. 15 to 30 second intervals (1500 or 3000) work well for boats and land based vehicles.

Line 3 sets the location of **dLOG2** backup files. A typical line would read

```
'c:\surveys\dlogba
```

The single quotes are necessary. As a guard against data loss, **dLOG2** will create backup data files when the diskette icon is pressed. The backup files will be stored in this location on your hard disk. **dLOG2** will not create this directory; you must specify an existing directory.

Before connecting up the GPS, it must be set to transmit NMEA standard output. The GPS unit should be set to transmit fixes as frequently as the unit will permit. The baud rate must match GPS.DAT.

dLOG2 Output

dLOG2 records information from the GPS, the internal time-clock of the computer, and user input (species observed, counts, etc.) into a single basic **dLOG2** output file. This file is saved each time the [Enter] key is pressed or a new GPS fix is acquired. When you exit **dLOG2**, three additional output files are created. If the basic output file is named **outputfile.txt**, the three additional output files are:

- **Outputfile.csv**
  This is the basic output file in a comma delimited format that can be read directly into Excel.

- **Outputfile_Obs.shp, Outputfile_Obs.DBF, Outputfile_Obs.SHX**

This is an ArcView Shape file of points. Each point represents one user-generated record, most commonly an observation of an animal or group of animals. Outputfile_Obs.DBF includes the Species (NAME) and the Count (CAMDAT).

- **Outputfile_Trk.shp, Outputfile_Trk.DBF, Outputfile_Trk.SHX**
  This is an ArcView Shape file of lines representing the survey track.

TECHNICAL DATA: Output Record Format

Data are written to the specified file each time the [Enter] key is pressed or a new GPS fix is acquired. The basic output file is an ASCII text in a fixed column format. The format definition is as follows:

Col.	1- 12	Latitude (decimal degrees)
	13- 24	Longitude (decimal degrees)
	25- 27	Hour (24 hour clock)
	28- 30	Minute
	31- 33	Second
	34- 38	Year
	39- 41	Month
	42- 44	Day
	45- 50	Record number
	51- 55	Data record type (GPS, USER, or START)
	56- 63	Distance to Marker (meters)
	64- 67	Heading to Marker (degrees)
	68- 75	Minimum distance to land (meters)
	76- 81	Depth (meters)

Up to 15 user fields follow. The contents of fields 1 through 15 is dependent on the field type set in the FIELDS.DAT file. Integer and real fields are right justified. The number of places after the decimal for real numbers are set in the FIELDS.DAT file. Alphameric fields are left justified. Mixed fields are separated into a 5 column integer and a 5 column text component. The integer field is on the right; the text field is on the left. The integer portion is right justified; the text portion is left justified.

R.Glenn Ford
R.G. Ford Consulting Company
2735 N.E. Weidler Street
Portland, OR 97232
September 2004

Observer Manual for Boat Surveys for Marine Birds

US Fish and Wildlife Service
Migratory Bird Management
March 2005

I. INTRODUCTION

A. Purpose

The purpose of this guide is to acquaint the reader with sampling protocols for Seabird and Marine Mammal Survey. This type of surveys began in 1989 in Prince William Sound and has been expanded to Southeast Alaska and Lower Cook Inlet. The PWS survey was designed by Steve Klowsiswoki. The Southeast Alaska and Lower Cook Inlet survey designs are similar to the Prince William Sound surveys except for the method in which transects are created, and the length of pelagic transects.

The Observer handbook was originally written by Laing and Burns for use in Prince William Sound (PWS). It has been updated to incorporated S.E. and LCI surveys techniques. In 1994, surveys were conducted in all three regions. These sampling techniques are somewhat complicated, so in order to be consistent with previous surveys, this handbook has been designed to give new observers a working knowledge of the survey techniques before entering the field.

B. Survey Organization

The 2005 survey activities will be under the direction of Kelsey Sullivan. Each survey vessel is staffed by a 3-person team consisting of a boat operator and 2 crew members. Responsibilities of the boat operators include daily survey logistics and data quality control. All members of the boat team participate in the navigation, piloting, observing, and data recording.

II. THE SURVEYS

A. Survey Dates:

The 2005 winter survey will be conducted from February 28 to March 20.

B. Transects

There are generally 3 classes of transects: shoreline, coastal-pelagic and pelagic. Survey technique for all types is similar, but each type of data is recorded in a different manner. On any transect, when the boat is moving, all birds and mammals are counted within the space that extends 100m each side, 100m ahead of, and 100m above the boat. Each survey has a list of transects with starting and ending points listed in latitude-longitude, or, as with PWS, shoreline transects are marked on nautical charts. Global Positioning Systems (GPS), large-scale computer-generated maps, lists of transect coordinates, and nautical charts are necessary to accurately locate transects.

C. Shoreline Transects

Survey Method
While the boat is moving, all birds and mammals are counted within the space that extends 100m each side, 100m ahead of, and 100m above the boat. The three-dimensional space created by these dimensions is known as the "sampling window."

Shoreline transects are surveyed at a distance of 100m from shore at a cruising speed of 5-10 kts. The inside observer surveys from the boat to the shore and 100 meters inland, while the outside observer surveys from the boat seaward an additional 100m. In this manner, the 200m strip adjacent to the shore is sampled in addition to a 100m shoreline strip. Figure 1 illustrates a typical shoreline transect. Transect 226 is located on the southeast side of Cabin Bay on Naked Island. The cross-hatched area represents the 200m wide strip that is sampled by the observers. Animals observed on the shoreline side are recorded as "side 1" while animals observed on the seaward side are recorded as "side 2."

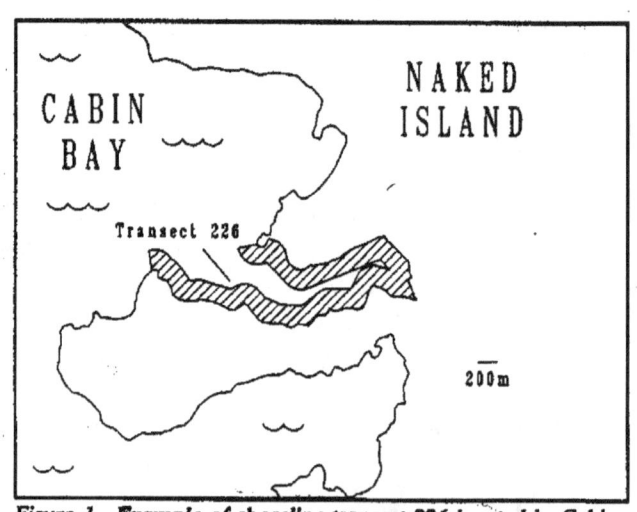

Prince William Sound
Shoreline transects in Prince William Sound are based on those of Irons, Nysewander, and Trapp (1988). This study serves as the pre-spill baseline data set for damage assessment. Transects are marked on nautical charts and large-scale computer generated maps.

S.E. Alaska
The shoreline transects are randomly selected using using a grid of 2 minutes longitude by 1 minute latitude overlay of the study area. Shoreline falling within the selected block is surveyed. If the shoreline transect is less than 0.5 miles it is merged with an adjacent block. Computer generated maps were produced for each shoreline transect to assist observer in delineating the starting and end points of each shoreline transects

Figure 1. Example of shoreline transect 226 located in Cabin Bay, Naked Island, Prince William Sound.

Lower Cook Inlet
The shoreline transects were randomly selected from a grid of 2 minutes latitude by 4 minutes longitude overlay of the study area. Shoreline falling within the selected block is surveyed. If the shoreline transect is less than 0.5 miles it is merged with an adjacent block. Computer generated maps were produced for each shoreline transect to assist observer in delineating the starting and end points of each shoreline transects

30

C. Offshore Transects

Survey Method

Areas greater than 200m from shore are sampled with similar methodology and sampling window (100m to either side, 100m ahead, and 100m above the boat). All pelagic sightings are recorded as "side 1;" however, where pelagic transects intersect with the 200m shoreline strip, data from within the shoreline zone are recorded as "side 2."

Prince William Sound

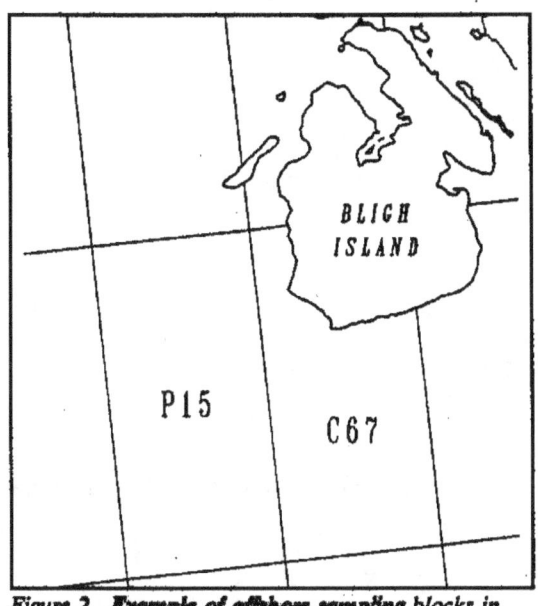

Figure 2. Example of offshore sampling blocks in Prince William Sound.

Prince William Sound survey blocks are based on a 5-minute latitude/longitude grid. This design was selected with the intention that aerial surveys would be conducted in conjunction with boat surveys. Blocks are classified as two types: "coastal/pelagic" blocks have more than 1 nautical mile of shoreline located within their boundaries, and "pelagic" blocks which have less than 1 nm of shoreline. Figure 2 illustrates an example of offshore sampling blocks P15 and C67. Block C67 is considered a coastal/pelagic because it contains more than 1nm of shoreline (on Bligh Island). Block P15 is considered pelagic because it is not adjacent to any land mass, and therefore has no shoreline. For continuity, 5 □ 5 grid cells were combined in some coastal/pelagic blocks.

The original survey design calls for 2 transects to be placed within each offshore block. However, some coastal/pelagic blocks have an odd number of transects due to the pooling mentioned earlier. Offshore transects are oriented true north-south along meridians located 1 minute of longitude inside the boundaries of the block. That is, if the east and west boundaries of a block are 147 30'W and 147 35'W, the transect lines for this block are at 147 31'W and 147 34'W. The two transect lines within offshore blocks are referred to as the east and west lines, respectively. Figure 3 illustrates pelagic block P17. The dashed line on the left is transect P17W; the one on the right P17E. In coastal/pelagic blocks with 3 transect lines, an additional transect identification number is added to differentiate between "east 1" and "east 2."

31

S.E. Alaska

All offshore transects in SE are called pelagic. These transects were randomly selected using a grid of 2 minutes longitude by 1 minute latitude. The transects run east west on the northern edge of the selected block. All pelagic transects are run on a given latitude with starting and ending point listed as longitude numbers. Pelagic transects range from 1 mile to 1/10 of a mile depending if the northern edge of the block hits land or not.

Lower Cook Inlet

All offshore transects are called pelagic transects. These transects were randomly selected using a grid of 2 minutes latitude by 4 minutes longitude. The north east corner of the grid block

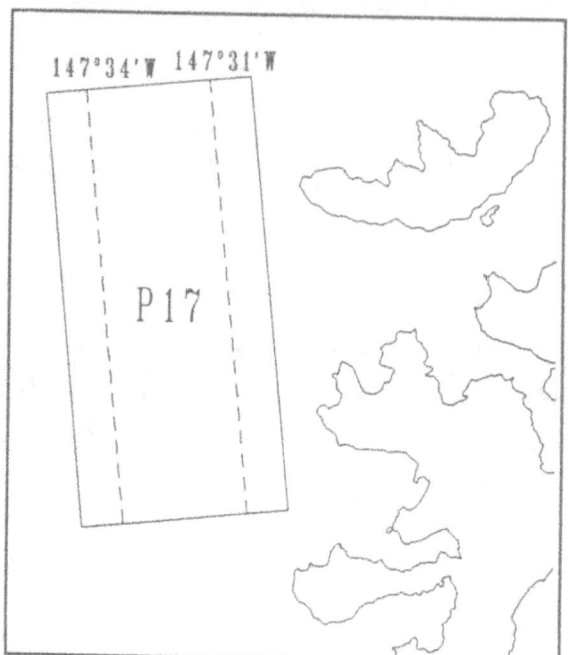

Figure 3. Example of meridians used for offshore transect lines.

was used as a starting point. Any transect that was □ 0.5 nautical miles was merged with an adjacent block. Transect range in length from 2.49 to 0.5 nautical mile. The transects intersecting land would run either north south or east west. Open water transects all ran north south.

D. Seasonal Changes In Surveys

Ideally the marine and coastal bird census are conducted in the summer and winter to count resident birds and avoid migrational flocks. Weather conditions and day light hours in the winter will limit the number of transects that can be done in a specific time period. Winter surveys may be designed as doing only a percentage of summer transects or use different transect and larger vessels.

III.   DATA RECORDING

Most of the data collected are entered directly into the dLOG2 program. We still use a paper data sheet to back up environmental data and logistical information, however. The dLOG2 program allows the data recorder to enter data into 15 fields; each field can contain both a numeric piece of information as well as an alphabetical piece. For example, a sighting of 12 marbled murrelets may be recorded as 12MAMU, MAMU12, MA12MU, or any other variation, so long as the characters appear in the correct order.

A. Transect Information

Prior to the start of each transect, environmental and observer data are collected. These data are also referred to as "header" information, since they were historically recorded at the top of a paper data sheet. Now this information is all that is recorded on the physical data sheet. Most of these data are also entered directly into the dLOG2 program. Since dLOG2 data are entered continuously throughout the transect, if conditions change over the course of the transect (e.g. sea conditions, ice cover, etc.), the recorder must update the information immediately in the correct field in dLOG2.

The following is an item-by-item description of the header data to be collected for each transect.

1. Transect ID

    Record on the header sheet as well as entering the transect number directly into dLOG2. At the top of the header sheet circle the type of transect, i.e. shoreline, pelagic, or coastal-pelagic. Record the survey transect number. For shoreline transect name begins with the letter 'S'. When you enter the transect ID into dLOG2, DO NOT pad this field with leading zeroes. For offshore transects, the complete alphanumeric transect number is recorded with no blanks, hyphens, slashes, or other embellishments.

CORRECT	INCORRECT
7	007
P70E	P 70 E
C188W	C-188-W

    Lower Cook Inlet
    We are experimenting with the pelagic transects of Lower Cook Inlet. To facilitate statistical analysis, break the transect into one mile segments (as determined by GPS), recording the first mile section as PNo#+A and the second mile section as PNo#+B. Do not stop to retake the header information for each mile section. The header information for both sections should be filled out at the beginning of the first mile section. Staple data sheets for each section together at the end of the day.

2. Observation Conditions

    Observation conditions is a single letter code, entered into a dLOG2 field along with "Weather" (see next) with valid codes listed on the "cheat sheet" in the survey binder. Conditions can range from "F" for fair to "O" for optimal. Factors affecting observation conditions include glare, wave action, precipitation, fog, etc. Assessment of observation conditions is somewhat subjective, but try to remain consistent. Always record as a single letter.

33

<u>CORRECT</u>	<u>INCORRECT</u>
O	O - R

3. Weather

Weather is recorded as a 2-digit numeric field in dLOG2, combined with "Observation Conditions" (see previous) with valid codes listed on the "cheat sheet" in the survey binder. This variable is simply the existing weather conditions in the general area of the transect. If two or more codes may apply, record the one that has the most profound effect on survey conditions. Example: if it is raining, do not record "03,68." The fact that it is raining implies cloud cover. Record this situation as "68." If a novel weather situation occurs for which no existing single weather code is applicable, write the conditions in the "comment" section of the header sheet. Upon return to camp, a new weather code can be created.

4. Date

Record the date on the header sheet. DLOG2 will automatically record the date in the data file. Each day's data file should be saved as the boat's 4-letter code plus that day's date in mddyy format. The file should also end in "a" – that way, if a new file is needed before the day's end, it can be the "b" file, etc.

Examples:
File for Scavenger on March 3 2005: SCAV30305a (if a second file is needed, use "b" to distinguish)
File for Predator on July 23 2005:   PRED72305a
File for Prey on February 28 2005:   PREY22805a

5. Time

Record the start time and end time of the transect in military (24-hour) time as hhmm on the header sheet. This is helpful for any editing that takes place later on. There is no need to enter the time into dLOG2; the program records the time automatically.

6. Wind Speed

In addition to recording the wind speed on the header sheet, also enter the speed into the dLOG2 data file. Wind speed and direction (see below) are recorded in the same dLOG2 field. Record the wind speed in miles per hour using the "kestrel" wind gauge. If no wind is detectable, record as "0" (do not leave blank). Decimal values are allowed, ranges are not.

<u>CORRECT</u>	<u>INCORRECT</u>
5.0	4kts
6.5	6-7

7. Wind Direction

In addition to recording the wind direction on the header sheet, also enter the direction into the dLOG2 data file. Wind direction and speed (see above) are recorded in the same dLOG2 field, so the direction MUST be recorded as a letter code: therefore, record the direction of the wind in compass direction. Smoke from the engines, or hanging a piece of toilet paper at arm's length can help determine direction of light winds. If wind is nonexistent, or variable, record the bearing as "NONE." Ranges are not allowed. Do not leave blank.

CORRECT	INCORRECT
NNW	185
NONE	0
SE	SE-SW

8. Vessel

The vessel name and the sea code (see below) are entered into the same field in dLOG2. Record the name of the survey vessel's four-letter code (PRED, PREY, SCAV, STAR, SESP, or SECO).

9. Seas

The sea code and the vessel name (see above) are entered into the same field in dLOG2. Record the Beaufort sea state code as a single-digit numeric value (see "cheat sheet" in survey binder for codes). Sea state, like observation conditions, is somewhat subjective. Again, try to remain consistent throughout the season. Decimals and ranges are not allowed. If conditions are truly borderline, record the higher of the two sea states.

CORRECT	INCORRECT
2	1-2
3	2.5

10. Inside Observer/Outside Observer

Record the three initials of each observer into the appropriate dLOG2 fields.

11. Salinity

Record the salinity of the water in parts per thousand. This should be determined by hanging the salinity meter overboard at a depth of 1 meter for at least 30 seconds. Decimals are allowed, ranges are not.

12. Turbidity (Secchi)

Record the turbidity of the water in meters. This should be determined by lowering the secchi disk straight down into the water until you can no longer distinguish the dark regions from the light regions. It is important to send the secchi disk as straight down as possible – the boat operator may have to use the engines to hold the boat still during the turbidity measurement. Decimals are allowed, ranges are not.

13. Human Disturbance Code

Record both on the header sheet as well as in the data file. Airplanes, helicopters, and other boats are also recorded as sighting events. The real concern with these objects is not necessarily their distribution and abundance, but rather their effect on the sampling of the transect. The disturbance code attempts to identify if the birds and beasts that inhabit a given area have been disturbed from their usual patterns of behavior. Valid disturbance codes are listed below. If no disturbance occurred, enter a "0." *If a disturbance code greater than 0 is entered, be sure to describe the disturbance in the comment section* (see below). You would be wholly correct to notice that our survey vessels are themselves a disturbance factor, but please do not record as such. Describe any disturbance in the comment section of the header sheet. If a disturbance becomes apparent partway through the transect, be sure to update the code in the dLOG2 field.

Code	Disturbance
0	No disturbance
1	Slight disturbance (1 or 2 small vessels/planes/people crossing part of the transect strip)
2	Several small v/p/p or 1 large vessel traveling over a significant portion of the transect strip over a significant chunk of the transect
3	Lots of v/p/p's covering much of the transect (e.g. near villages or fishing hotspots)

14. Ice Type

Record the ice type on the header sheet. Ice type and cover (see below) are entered into the same dLOG2 field. Record the ice type as a single letter code ("G" for glacial or "S" for sheet ice). If both types are present, record the predominant type. If no ice is present, record as "N." Do not leave this field blank.

15. Ice Cover

Record the percent ice cover on the header sheet. Ice cover and type (see above) are entered into the same dLOG2 field. Record the total surface area of the transect that is covered by ice to the nearest 10% (0-100%). If no ice is present, record as "0." Decimals and ranges are not allowed. Do not leave blank. If possible, draw a picture of the transect and ice cover on the back of the data sheet.

16. Air Temperature

Record the air temperature in degrees Celsius. This should be determined by holding a thermometer in air for at least 30 seconds. Make sure the thermometer is dry, and not in the sunlight or wind.

17. Water Temperature

Record the water temperature in degrees Celsius. Read the water temperature measured by the salinity meter during the salinity measurements (see "salinity" above). Decimals are allowed, ranges are not.

18. Comments

Record any general comments for that transect on the header sheet. These could include comments on disturbance factors, locations of eagle nests, equipment problems that interrupt survey effort, etc. Leave blank if no comments are necessary. Comments for a S.E. Alaska transect guide are especially needed to create a transect guide for that area.

Comments can also be recorded in dLOG2 – only about 8 characters will fit in the field, so if you are entering a longer comment, continually hit "enter" to start a new line in the data file.

19. Edits

If you realize that you've made an error in data entry at any point during a transect, IMMEDIATELY write the time and identifying information about the entry in the "edit" area on the header sheet for that transect. Record the correct information so that the entry can later be changed. ** It is possible to edit the dLOG2 file in the field, but ONLY edit non-repeating fields, like comments and sighting information. NEVER try to edit the repeating fields (transect ID, environmental data, etc.).

B. Sighting Information

> After the header information has been recorded and the survey vessel is "on transect," the outside observer/data recorder records all bird and mammal sightings directly into the dLOG2 file.

Species

> "Species/number" is the first field on the dLOG2 screen. Enter the four-letter species code for each sighting into this field, as well as the number of animals in the group (see "number" below). The most commonly observed species are listed by species code on the cheat sheet in the survey binder. If you cannot find the species in the list of codes, enter "XXXX" into the species field. **Write the full name of these species** on the header sheet so that the correct code can later be entered.

Number

> In the same field, enter the number of animals in the group. By default, if you enter no number, dLOG2 will record the number of animals as "1."

Behavior

> The next field is "behavior/side." The behavior code is used to represent whether the animal was on land, water, or in the air at the time of sighting. One exception to this happens when the animal flies up from behind and proceeds ahead in the same direction as the survey vessel. This behavior is considered "following." Another exception is animals sitting or standing on floating objects (buoys, logs, icebergs, etc.); for this situation, use the "float" code. Use the sighting modifier that represents the location of the animal at the moment you first see the animal. If you see 2 marbled murrelets (MAMU) flying up ahead of the boat, do not infer that they were probably sitting on the water. Record this sighting as 2 MAMUs in air. Call them as you see them. For this reason, the 1989 data base contains a single record of a humpback whale in the air. SEE **HOTKEYS** BELOW.

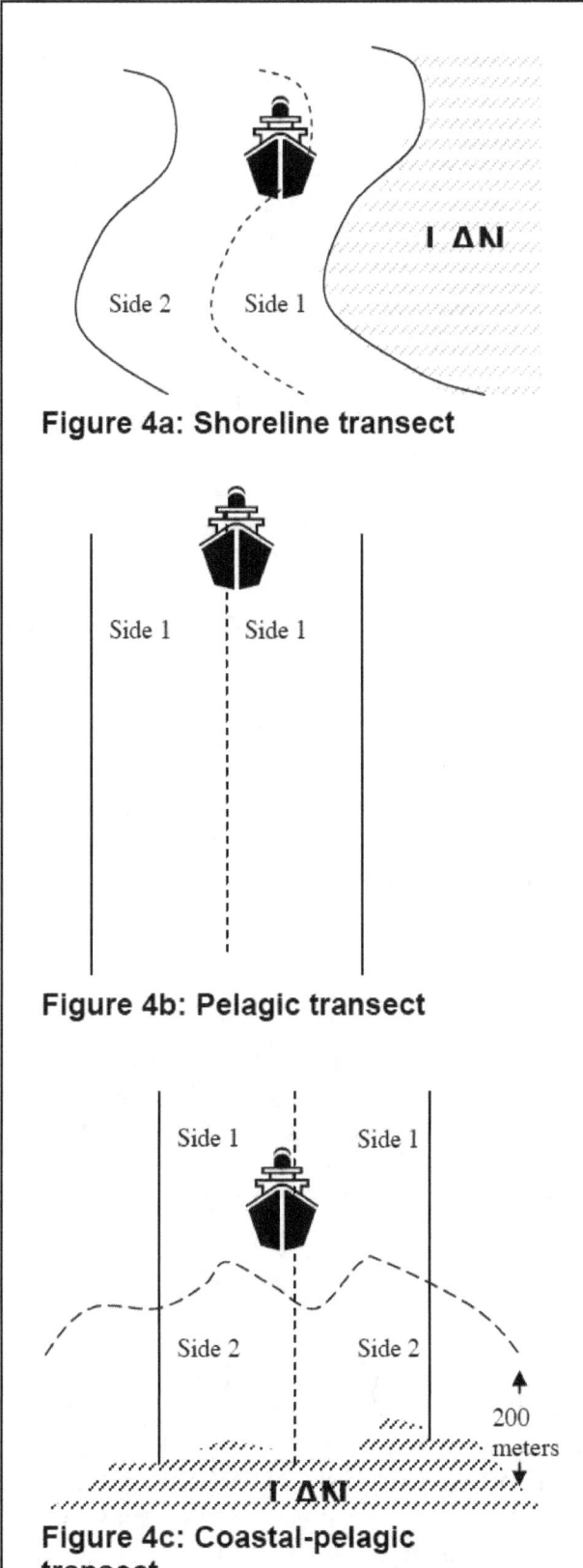

Figure 4a: Shoreline transect

Figure 4b: Pelagic transect

Figure 4c: Coastal-pelagic
~~transect~~

Side

For shoreline surveys, record sightings as the appropriate side ("side 1" is the shoreline side and "side 2" is the seaward side) (Figure 4a). For pelagic and coastal-pelagic surveys, "side 1" is used to record all birds and mammals observed at a distance greater than 200m from shore. "Side 2" is used to record all birds and mammals observed within 200m of the shore (Figure 4b&c). SEE **HOTKEYS** BELOW

HOTKEYS
For the behavior/side field, there are a number of shortcut "hotkeys" available. By pressing one of the function keys, you can enter both the behavior and the side data with a single keystroke. Refer to the list of hotkeys in the dLOG2 instructions in the survey binder. They may also be labeled on your computer's keyboard.

When observing cormorants, UNCO should be used only when you cannot tell whether the bird is a double-crested or pelagic/red-faced. If the cormorant is not a double-crested and it cannot be determined whether it is a pelagic or a red-faced, it should be recorded as PRCO. Hint: Double crested cormorants are larger, more stocky appearing and have thicker necks than red faced or pelagic cormorants.

Sea otter pups require an additional note. If a mother/pup pair are sighted, record it as 2SEOT and write in the comment field "1 pup." If a group of 7 adult otters, 2 with pups is sighted, record as 9SEOT and write in the comments "2 pups."

Understand that while the boat is moving and the inside observer and driver are calling out sightings; the outside observer has the double responsibility of observing and data recording. It can get hectic. However, *the importance of recording data accurately cannot be understated*. If you suspect you may have mistyped a sighting, IMMEDIATELY record the time and what the entry should be in the "edit" section of the header sheet.

Make any corrections at the end of each and every day! Share this responsibility fairly among the crew.

C.   Unique Situations

On paper, the survey methodology is fairly straightforward. However, in the field, situations arise that have raised certain questions in the past. For instance: if a gull is flying really high along the side of a hill, is it counted or not? This section will attempt to resolve some of the more common questions encountered while surveying.

1.   Sampling Window - spatial

The purpose of the survey is to count birds and otters, and many observers feel compelled to record *every* bird and otter they see, disregarding the boundaries of the sampling window. Exercise discipline, and avoid extending the sampling window to include sightings. If in doubt, ask the driver or other observer for their opinion. It seems rather obvious, but once and for all: *If a bird or otter is not within the sampling window, do not record it!* (Just say NO).

2.   Sampling Window - temporal

The ideal way to conduct a census or survey of animal populations would be to take a snapshot of the entire study area at a single point in time. This would allow you to count every animal present within the study area and eliminate the possibility of double-counting individuals. Obviously this is impossible, so an approximation of this method is required. The solution is to sample a survey "window" that is moving through space and time. In order to approximate the instantaneous nature of a snapshot, the window would ideally be sampled for a split-second, then the boat would move on. Again, this is not practical, and is approximated by moving the boat along the transect at a relatively constant velocity. Problems arise when the boat comes to a stop. This can happen for a variety of reasons: mechanical problems, difficult species identifications, counting large groups of birds at colonies, etc. For the purposes of this study, *if the boat has stopped moving for any reason, the sampling window is closed.*

To fully understand this concept, imagine you are stopped at a salmon stream to count a large group of gulls. If you are stopped for one minute and count fly-throughs, you introduce a slight positive bias to your count for the transect. However, if you sit at the stream for an hour and count fly-throughs, you introduce a larger bias to your count. As in section III.C.1. above, the purpose of the survey is not to record every single bird and mammal that you see, but rather to conduct a statistically valid sample of these animals within the study area.

3. Rocks

Animals located on rocks are recorded as animals on land. A problem arises when a rock is located more than 100m from the shoreline. A general rule of thumb is: if the rock appears to be exposed at mean high water (MHW), consider it as shoreline, and record the sighting as "side 1." Small islands fit this description well. If the rock appears to be covered at high water, record the sighting on the right side of the data sheet. This situation gives rise to the seemingly cryptic description of an animal located greater than 100m from shore, on land.

4. Ice

Bearing in mind that ice was what started this whole thing, there are a few comments about ice located within transects. The first is a general rule of thumb put forth by Greg Balogh: *if an iceberg is large enough that you would rather not have it dropped on your head, then don't hit it with the boat.* The second point deals with ice that obstructs survey of the transect. If ice prevents your ability to adequately see portions of the transect, estimate the percentage of the transect area that cannot be surveyed and record this value in the comments section of the data sheet. Remember to draw a picture of the ice coverage on the back of the data sheet. The estimate of the area that cannot be surveyed and a map can be used to calculate a correction factor for the unsurveyed habitat.

*** If ice prevents the boat from traveling part of the transect course BUT you can still scan the actual transect line with reasonable accuracy, record sightings as if the boat were on the actual transect track. Make a note on the header sheet whenever this procedure is necessary.

5. Flushing and Diving

The question of animals that flush or dive ahead of the boat comes down a single point: did that activity of the survey vessel cause the animal to alter its behavior? If so, then record the animal(s) on the data sheet. The only rule is to use good judgement and common sense. Bald eagles (BAEA) are not nailed to trees; they come and go of their own free will. If an eagle sighted in a tree several hundred meters ahead of the boat takes flight, do not automatically assume that your boat was the cause. He may have just gone off to feed. This is a subjective decision on the part of the individual observer. Feel free to discuss the situation with the other crew members. The final call should go to the observer who made the sighting in the first place.

6. Rollup

A special case of flushing is known as rollup. This occurs when birds flushed by the survey vessel fly ahead and land farther along in the transect. These animals could then be counted multiple times, depending on their behavior and the length of the transect. Again, use common sense. If a flock of 12 harlequin ducks (HARD) flush forward into the transect, and immediately around the next bend you sight "another" flock of 12 HARDs, consider the possibility that they are the same flock.

An additional confounding situation would be if in the example presented above, the second flock contained 17 HARDs. At least 5 more HARDs are present on the transect than were seen previously. This situation should be recorded as a new sighting of 17 HARDs, or the original 12 *plus* an additional sighting of 5.

7. Species Identification

Several assumptions should be avoided while identifying an animal to species.

The first is when you can ID a bird to the level of genus perhaps (murrelet, murre, cormorant, etc.) but not to species. Avoid saying: it was a murre, and since common murres are more abundant in Prince William Sound than thick-billed murres, it must have been a common murre. *If you aren't sure*, then record it as an unknown murre. Assuming the species based on relative abundance may only serve to perpetuate the illusion that one species is more abundant than the other. The most common occurrence of this is with marbled murrelets (MAMU) and Kittlitz's murrelet (KIMU). If you do not see adequate field marks, do not assume it is a MAMU. Record it as an identified murrelet of the genus *Brachyramphus* (BRMU).

The second situation occurs when mixed flocks are counted. If there are 25 gulls on a rock, and 22 of them are positively identified as mew gulls (MEGU), but the

42

remaining 3 gulls are obscured so no field marks can be seen, do not assume them to be MEGUs. Record those 3 as unidentified gulls (UNGU). If you aren't satisfied with that identification, then maneuver the boat for a better view so you can see field marks. The exception to this rule is for waterfowl. Often, hens are difficult to identify to species. However, if a flock of hens and drakes are sighted, it is relatively safe to count them all as the same species.

8. Distance Inland

The primary objective of this survey is not to record terrestrial animals. However, non-target species that are sighted should be recorded. Do not record sightings of animals that are greater than 100m inland from the shoreline. This includes birds located far upstream, or bald eagles (BAEA) soaring or perched in trees well inland. If you make a really spectacular sighting of a terrestrial mammal that doesn't belong on the data sheet and feel you have to tell someone about it, record it in the comments section.

9.3 Appendix C. Techniques for shipboard surveys of marine birds. 1989. P.J. Gould and D.J. Forsell. Technical Report US Fish and Wildlife Service. 25 pp.

9.4 Appendix D. Field identification of Kittlitz's Murrelet.

9.5 Appendix E. Data Forms and Data Dictionaries

Transect Log
Example of a transect log sheet used during marine birds and mammals surveys

Transect
no._22_____   MB&M Survey
                           recorder__**JBodkin**_____   Page _____

Survey Date: _dd/mm/year (ex:13072006)_____

Season (circle one): __Winter_____Summer____

Format for Naming .SRV output files: example:_AP 10 13072006 22 w_____

Region: _AP_____Block no._10_____

Date	Boat Name	Transect #	File Name	Start Time	Stop Time	Proofed	Comments

Please be accurate with times.

Please cross-off comments if fixed during proofing.

Data dictionary for data fields in Table 2 Transect Log

Header data

Transect number: List numerical number of transect.

Marine birds and mammals survey recorder: Make master list with full names of observers and recorders. Record first initial and full last name of recorder, example: JBodkin = Jim Bodkin.

Page: List as page 1 of 1.

Survey Date: day/month/year :(dd/mm/year) 13072006 = 13 of July, 2006.

Season (circle one): You must circle to indicate which season. Seasonal surveys are conducted the same month every year, winter = March and summer = June or July.

Format for Naming SRV output files: File names will include the 2-3 character code for the region being surveyed (e.g. PWS, KP, KOD, and AP), the 1-2 character number of the intensive block (1-15) if applicable, followed by the date (day/month/year: dd/mm/year), the transect number (up to 3 numbers), followed by the season (w for winter, and s for summer). As an example AP 10 13072006 22 S.srv represents the file name assigned to transect 22 in the intensive block 10 along the Alaska Peninsula coast sampled on 13 July 2006.

Region: the N-REM region in which the data were collected: **PWS** (Prince William Sound), **KP** (Kenai Peninsula), **KOD** (Kodiak), or **AP** (Alaska Peninsula).

Block number: List block number numerically

Tabular data

Date: day/month/year (dd/mm/year)

Boat name: list name of boat and include registration number if using a small inflatable.

Transect #: List numerical number of transect.

File name: AP 10 13072006 22 S = Region, block #, date, transect # and season. This log is used to verify transect data in dLOG2 and to make note of errors that will later require editing of electronic files. File names will include the 2-3 character code for the region being surveyed (e.g. PWS, KP, KOD, and AP), the 1-2 character number of the intensive block (1-12) if applicable, followed by the date (day/month/year: dd/mm/year), the transect number (up to 3 numbers), followed by the season (w for winter, and s for summer). As an example AP 10 13072006 22 S.srv represents the file name assigned to transect 22 in the intensive block 10 along the Alaska Peninsula coast sampled on 13 July 2006.

Start time: military time "18:45". **Accurate recording of start and stop transect times and transect numbers are essential.** It may be necessary to go "off transect" prior to completing a transect (e.g. to identify and count a complex flock of birds or a rare marine mammal, or for other navigational purposes). The transect log should be used to record these times as well as using the "off "and "on" transect keys in dLOG2.

Stop time: military time "20:30". **Accurate recording of start and stop transect times and transect numbers are essential.** It may be necessary to go "off transect" prior to completing a transect (e.g. to identify and count a complex flock of birds or a rare marine mammal, or for other navigational purposes). The transect log should be used to record these times as well as using the "off "and "on" transect keys in dLOG2.

Proofed: At the end of each day data sheets should be proofed and edited to reflect any changes. A check mark with your initials (first letters of your first, middle and last name, e.g. JLB) is to be entered in the proofed column on each data sheet.

Comments: Comments on unusual sightings or occurrences are encouraged and can be entered directly into the dLOG2 comments field or in the transect log to later be appended to the transect data file. Cross-off comments and initial (first letters of your first, middle and last name, e.g. JLB) if fixed during proofing.

NPS 953/107687, May 2011

www.ingramcontent.com/pod-product-compliance
Lightning Source LLC
Chambersburg PA
CBHW081136290526
45795CB00006B/2265